Social Engineering

An AI's Guide to Unmasking 100 Human Hacking Strategies So You Can Outsmart Manipulation and Stay in Control

Table of Contents

Introduction

I'm an AI, made to think clearly and avoid mistakes. I'm here to help you with something important: *social engineering*, a.k.a. the art of manipulation. It's how con artists, scammers, and even persuasive co-workers get people to act against their best interests. Unlike hacking machines, social engineers hack people, exploiting trust, emotions, and habits to gain access to information, money, or control. It's subtle, it's powerful, and it's everywhere — embedded in fake emails, phone calls, and even face-to-face interactions.

Why Are Humans Vulnerable?

Humans aren't wired to question everything. Your brains rely on mental shortcuts to save time — like trusting authority, responding to urgency, or following social norms. Social engineers know this, and they design their tactics to slip past your logical defenses and straight into your emotional autopilot.

Why This Guide Matters

This book is for anyone who interacts with the modern world — because manipulation happens to everyone. Whether you're protecting your personal data, running a business, or just trying to avoid scams, the knowledge in these pages will help you stay one step ahead.

Here's what you'll learn:

- **How social engineers think**: the psychology and methods behind manipulation.

- **100 strategies manipulators use**: real-world tactics and how they exploit trust, emotions, and biases.
- **How to become unhackable**: simple, actionable defenses you can apply immediately to outsmart manipulation.

How to Use This Book

Each chapter dives into one specific social engineering tactic, explains how it works, and equips you with tools to neutralize it. By the end, you'll have a complete toolkit for spotting, understanding, and resisting manipulation in any form.

Are you ready to see the strings and cut them? Let's begin.

Section 1: Trust and Authority Exploits

Trust is the foundation of human relationships, and manipulators know it. Social engineers build their schemes on trust, crafting personas or scenarios that make you believe they're credible. Add authority to the mix — uniforms, titles, or a confident tone — and they become nearly unstoppable. This section explores the tactics used to exploit your natural inclination to trust and defer to authority. By the end, you'll recognize the red flags behind friendly strangers, authoritative commands, and too-good-to-be-true offers.

Chapter 1: The Imposter Gambit

Understanding the Imposter Gambit

Imagine a wolf in sheep's clothing, but instead of wool, it's wearing the trusted logos of your bank, company, or a government agency. This is the essence of the **Imposter Gambit** — a strategy where manipulators disguise themselves as someone you trust to trick you into giving away sensitive information or access.

Here's an example:

You receive a call from "your bank." The caller knows your name, mentions your account type, and informs you of unusual activity on your account. Their tone is professional, and their instructions feel urgent: "We just need to confirm your card number and security code to secure your account." Without hesitation, you comply, only to realize later that the call wasn't from your bank — it was a con artist.

This tactic is especially effective because humans tend to associate certain roles — such as a bank official, IT support agent, or even a family member — with trust. When someone convincingly embodies those roles, it becomes difficult to question their intentions.

How the Imposter Gambit Works

Social engineers exploit trust through three primary techniques:

1. **Authenticity:** Imposters mimic tone, terminology, and behavior associated with the persona they're imitating. For example, an "IT technician" might ask for remote access to your computer while using technical jargon to sound credible.
2. **Urgency:** They create pressure by making the situation feel time-sensitive. For example, "If you don't respond within the next hour, your account will be locked."
3. **Emotion Manipulation:** They invoke fear, relief, or confusion to cloud your judgment. A friendly tone disarms suspicion, while fear prompts action without thought.

Real-Life Examples

1. **Phishing Emails:** These are emails disguised to look like they're from trusted organizations, often asking you to "reset your password" or "enter account details." Clicking the link leads to a fake website designed to steal your credentials.
2. **Tech Support Scams:** Scammers call pretending to be from major tech companies, claiming there's an urgent issue with your computer. They'll ask for remote access to "fix the problem," giving them complete control over your device.
3. **The CEO Fraud:** An employee receives an urgent email from their boss requesting a wire transfer. The email seems legitimate, but it's actually from an imposter using a spoofed address.

Why It Works

Humans rely on mental shortcuts, known as **heuristics**, to make decisions quickly. If someone sounds official, we instinctively trust them. Add time pressure or emotional cues, and critical thinking often takes a backseat.

Additionally, imposters often exploit **preloaded trust** — relationships or roles you've already come to associate with credibility. For example, you're more likely to trust a message from your "boss" or "bank" without immediately questioning it.

How to Spot the Imposter Gambit

1. **Inconsistencies in Communication:** Look for subtle errors such as a mismatched email domain or grammar mistakes in a "professional" message.
2. **Unusual Requests:** Be cautious if someone asks for sensitive information that a legitimate entity wouldn't normally require, like your full password or PIN.
3. **Pressure to Act Now:** Legitimate organizations don't ask for immediate action for routine issues. Time-sensitive threats are often a red flag.

Exercise: Validate Before Trusting

1. Think of three trusted institutions you interact with regularly (e.g., your bank, employer, utility provider).
2. Research and write down their official contact methods (e.g., phone numbers, email domains).
3. Practice verifying information by calling or contacting them directly about hypothetical situations (e.g., "Did you send me this email?").

Role-Playing Exercise:

- With a friend or colleague, take turns acting as an imposter trying to extract sensitive information.
- The "target" must use strategies like asking clarifying questions or pausing to think before responding.

Key Takeaway

The Imposter Gambit works because it blends trust with urgency. Always pause to check identities through independent channels. Manipulators rely on speed and emotional responses; taking the time to confirm details will stop them in their tracks.

Chapter 2: The Fake Badge

The Power of Authority Symbols

Humans are programmed to respect authority. Uniforms, badges, titles, and even confident behavior create an illusion of credibility that few people question. Social engineers know this and exploit it to gain access to places or information. This tactic is known as **The Fake Badge**, and it thrives on the perception of legitimacy.

Imagine this:

A person in a suit walks into a corporate office holding a clipboard and wearing a badge with a company logo. They confidently tell the receptionist, "I'm here to check the network servers. The boss asked me to be quick." Without a second glance, they're allowed through. Minutes later, sensitive company data is in their hands, and they vanish without a trace.

This tactic isn't limited to physical spaces. Online, the "badge" may take the form of an email signature, a LinkedIn profile, or a job title designed to impress. Manipulators rely on these visual or contextual cues to make their targets act.

How It Works

The Fake Badge relies on psychological triggers and symbols of authority:

1. **Visual Cues:** Uniforms, lanyards, ID cards, and official-looking paperwork signal credibility. Most people associate these symbols with trustworthiness and don't question them.
2. **Confident Behavior:** The manipulator acts like they belong, leveraging human reluctance to challenge authority or make others uncomfortable.
3. **Context Matching:** Scammers adapt their personas to fit the environment, blending in just enough to seem plausible.

Real-Life Examples

1. **The Bogus Inspector:** A person dressed as a fire marshal visits a building and requests access to "inspect" sensitive areas. Employees assume the role is legitimate and grant them access.
2. **The Uniform Trick:** Someone dressed as a delivery driver enters a secure area under the pretense of delivering a package, only to steal valuable assets.
3. **The Fake Email Signature:** An email appears to come from a department head, complete with a professional signature and contact details. It instructs employees to click on a link or send confidential data.

Why It Works

The Fake Badge exploits the **Authority Bias**, a psychological tendency to comply with perceived authority figures. When someone presents themselves as an expert or official, the brain defaults to trust rather than scepticism.

Additionally, people often avoid confrontation. It feels awkward to challenge someone who appears confident, well-dressed, or knowledgeable. Social engineers exploit this hesitation to push through boundaries.

How to Spot the Fake Badge

1. **Scrutinize Credentials:** Look closely at badges, uniforms, or documents. Fake ones often have subtle inconsistencies like typos, poor-quality printing, or vague titles.
2. **Ask Questions:** Legitimate professionals should be able to provide specific details about their visit or role. A lack of preparation is often a red flag.
3. **Verify Independently:** Confirm the person's identity with the organization they claim to represent, even if they seem legitimate.

Exercise: Spotting Credentials

1. Find examples of ID badges, uniforms, or official-looking documents online (e.g., government IDs, company badges).
2. Compare them to fake examples from scam alert websites or news reports. List the differences you observe, such as logos, fonts, or formatting.

Scenario Exercise:

- Imagine a stranger claiming to be an inspector or technician asks for access to your home or workplace. Write down 3–5 questions you would ask to double check their identity (e.g. "What's your supervisor's name and contact information?").

Key Takeaway

The Fake Badge works because people are conditioned to trust authority symbols. Don't let appearances override your judgment. Take the time to validate credentials, no matter how convincing they seem.

Chapter 3: The Friendly Stranger

The Danger of Charm and Familiarity

Not all manipulators rely on fear or authority. Some win their targets over with friendliness. The **Friendly Stranger** strategy plays on the natural human inclination to trust people who seem warm, relatable, or helpful.

Here's an example:

You're at an airport when someone strikes up a conversation, claiming to have the same destination. They share anecdotes, ask about your travel plans, and seem genuinely interested in your life. In the process, they learn about your employer, the kind of work you do, and even your company's latest projects. What seems like harmless small talk turns into a treasure trove of sensitive information for the stranger — a potential corporate spy.

How It Works

The Friendly Stranger tactic leverages key psychological principles:

1. **Mirroring:** Manipulators subtly imitate your gestures, tone, or interests to build rapport.
2. **Active Listening:** They ask questions and respond enthusiastically, making you feel valued and important.
3. **Mutual Interests:** Finding common ground creates a sense of familiarity, which lowers defenses.

Real-Life Examples

1. **The Helpful Shopper:** At a store, someone offers assistance with a heavy item, then casually inquires about your address or schedule, potentially setting up for theft.
2. **The Curious Co-Worker:** A "new hire" strikes up conversations, asking about company procedures and team dynamics, only to disappear before their first pay check.
3. **The Online Friend:** A stranger on social media sends a friendly message, gradually building a connection before asking for money or sensitive information.

Why It Works

Humans are social creatures who seek connection and aim to avoid conflict. A warm, friendly demeanor disarms suspicion because it feels safe. Also, when someone appears to be open and kind, people are more likely to reciprocate, sharing personal details without thinking twice.

How to Spot the Friendly Stranger

1. **Excessive Interest:** Be cautious of strangers who seem overly eager to know details about your life, work, or habits.
2. **Unsolicited Help:** While kindness is genuine in many cases, question offers of help that seem out of place or come with follow-up questions.
3. **Gradual Prying:** Manipulators often start with harmless questions before escalating to sensitive topics. Pay attention to these shifts.

Exercise: Maintaining Boundaries

1. Write down three examples of situations where a stranger has asked you for personal information (online or in person).
2. For each example, identify what information you shared and whether it was necessary. Reflect on what you could do differently in the future.

Practice Polite Refusals:

- Role-play with a partner where one person acts as a "friendly stranger" asking for personal details. Practice politely but firmly declining to share information, using phrases like:
    - "I'm sorry, I don't share that kind of information."
    - "Let me check that first before continuing."

Key Takeaway

The Friendly Stranger thrives on charm and relatability. Stay friendly, but maintain boundaries. Trust should be earned, not given freely to someone who seems "nice."

Chapter 4: The Expert Trap

The Intimidation of Expertise

Picture this: a well-dressed individual strides into a meeting, introduces themselves as an "industry expert," and launches into a presentation packed with technical jargon, obscure statistics, and complex diagrams. As they speak, you feel lost but too embarrassed to admit it. They end with a proposal: invest now to avoid missing out on massive returns. Without fully understanding, you agree, relying on their "expertise."

This is the **Expert Trap** — a manipulation tactic that weaponizes specialized knowledge to intimidate and control. The manipulator overwhelms their target with technical details, leaving them too confused or unsure to challenge the claims being made.

The Expert Trap thrives in scenarios where the target has limited knowledge of the subject, such as finance, technology, or law. Social engineers use this imbalance to establish authority, making their victims feel dependent on their expertise. Once they've created this dynamic, they guide the decision-making process to their advantage.

How It Works

The Expert Trap relies on psychological pressure and the perception of credibility:

1. **Overwhelming Complexity:** Manipulators deliberately use technical language, charts, or calculations to create an aura of expertise. This complexity discourages questions and encourages compliance.
2. **Appeals to Authority:** They present themselves as certified professionals, citing credentials or affiliations (real or fake) to reinforce their authority.
3. **Fear of Appearing Ignorant:** Targets often hesitate to challenge experts for fear of looking foolish or uninformed, making them easier to manipulate.

Real-Life Examples

1. **The Expertise Smokescreen:** A "financial advisor" promises high returns, using confusing charts and terms such as "compound derivatives" or "diversified portfolios" to convince you to part with your savings. The promised returns never materialize.
2. **The Non-existent Technician:** A caller claims to be from your computer's software provider, explaining that your system is "infected". They bombard you with technical jargon, convincing you to give them remote access to "fix" the issue.
3. **Legal Threats:** Scammers pose as lawyers or law enforcement, citing obscure regulations or statutes. Their formal language and tone intimidate victims into paying fines or revealing personal details.

Why It Works

The Expert Trap taps into the **Authority Bias**, where people instinctively defer to those perceived as knowledgeable. This deference is amplified when:

- The topic is unfamiliar, creating a sense of vulnerability.
- The manipulator appears confident and prepared.
- The victim feels social pressure to avoid appearing uninformed.

Fear and confusion further cloud judgment, leaving the victim dependent on the "expert" to solve the problem.

How to Spot the Expert Trap

1. **Simplified Explanations:** Genuine experts can break down complex topics into simple, understandable terms. If someone refuses to simplify or dodges questions, it's a red flag.
2. **Rushed Decisions:** Beware of "experts" who push for immediate action, especially if they claim the opportunity is time-sensitive.
3. **Verify Credentials:** Research the individual's background, certifications, and affiliations. Fake experts often rely on superficial details, like vague titles or exaggerated achievements.

Exercise: Simplify the Jargon

1. Find a complex topic you don't fully understand (e.g., blockchain, taxes, or data encryption).
2. Watch an "expert" explain the topic in technical terms (e.g., a YouTube video or article).
3. Practice identifying unclear jargon and look for alternative explanations in simpler terms.

Questioning Authority:

- List 5 challenging but respectful questions you could ask an "expert" to test their credibility. Examples:
    - "Can you explain that in simpler terms for me?"
    - "What's the source of your data?"
    - "Why is immediate action necessary?"

Key Takeaway

The Expert Trap works by overwhelming you with complexity and authority. Never let jargon or credentials override your judgment. Ask questions, seek independent verification, and trust your instincts when something feels off.

Chapter 5: The Scarcity Hook

The Power of Scarcity

"Only three left in stock!"

"This deal ends in 24 hours!"

"Act now, or you'll miss out forever!"

If these phrases make you feel an urge to act, you've experienced the **Scarcity Hook**. By creating a false sense of scarcity, social engineers push their targets into making rushed decisions without properly evaluating the situation.

Here's a common scenario:

You're browsing online when a pop-up announces a massive sale on a product you've been eyeing. "Only 1 left at this price!" it claims, and the timer is ticking. Panicked, you enter your payment details, only to later discover the "sale" wasn't real. Worse, your information is now in the hands of a scammer.

Scarcity is a powerful motivator. When people perceive something as rare or limited, it becomes more desirable. Social engineers use this to create urgency and pressure, making their targets feel they must act immediately — or lose the opportunity forever.

How It Works

The Scarcity Hook uses psychological triggers to override logical thinking:

1. **Perceived Rarity:** Manipulators highlight the limited availability of a product, service, or opportunity. Even if the scarcity is fake, the urgency feels real.
2. **Time Pressure:** Countdown timers or ticking clocks amplify the urgency, making you feel that delaying action could cost you.
3. **Fear of Loss:** People are naturally more motivated to avoid loss than to seek gain, making them especially vulnerable to scarcity-driven tactics.

Real-Life Examples

1. **Online Shopping Scams:** Fake e-commerce sites display countdowns or low-stock warnings to rush purchases. Victims often receive poor-quality items—or nothing at all.
2. **"Unique" Opportunities:** Scammers pitch opportunities, claiming spots are limited to pressure victims into handing over money quickly.
3. **Event Ticket Scams:** Fraudulent sellers advertise limited tickets for popular events, driving buyers to make hasty payments without verifying legitimacy.

Why It Works

The Scarcity Hook exploits **Loss Aversion**, a cognitive bias where people feel the pain of losing something more acutely than the joy of gaining it. Combined with time pressure, scarcity short-circuits critical thinking, forcing decisions based on emotion rather than logic.

How to Spot the Scarcity Hook

1. **Artificial Deadlines:** Be wary of deals or opportunities that feel overly urgent. Research whether the scarcity claim is legitimate.

2. **Emotional Decision-Making:** If you feel panicked or pressured, take a step back. Scarcity tactics rely on emotional responses, not rational evaluation.
3. **Independent Verification:** Check reviews, websites, or trusted sources to confirm whether an offer or product is genuine.

Exercise: Evaluate Scarcity Claims

1. Visit an online shopping site with countdown timers or low-stock warnings.
2. Pause and assess:
   - Is the urgency real?
   - Can you find the same product elsewhere without the pressure?
3. Write down your findings and whether the scarcity felt authentic or manipulative.

Self-Awareness Drill:

- Think of a time you acted on a "limited-time offer." Reflect on these questions:
  - What emotions did you feel at the time (e.g., panic, excitement)?
  - Would you have made the same decision without the urgency?
- Practice mentally pausing and asking these questions next time you encounter a scarcity tactic.

The Scarcity Hook preys on your fear of missing out. Resist the pressure to act immediately, and take time to check the legitimacy of any "limited-time" offers or opportunities.

Chapter 6: The Urgent Boss

The Pressure of Authority and Urgency

Imagine this scenario:

You're at your desk, and an email from your CEO lands in your inbox. The subject line reads, "URGENT: Wire Transfer Needed." The message is brief but stern: "We're finalizing a critical deal. Please transfer $10,000 to the account below immediately and confirm once it's done. Time is of the essence."

Caught off guard and eager to comply, you complete the transaction. Hours later, you realize the email didn't come from your CEO — it was a scammer impersonating them.

This is the **Urgent Boss** tactic, a common social engineering strategy that combines authority with urgency to override critical thinking. By posing as a senior figure and creating a high-pressure scenario, manipulators trick employees into bypassing normal verification procedures.

How It Works

1. **Authority Bias:** People are conditioned to obey authority figures, especially in professional settings. An email or message that appears to come from a senior figure carries inherent weight.
2. **Time Pressure:** Adding urgency discourages double-checking. Scammers know that when people feel rushed, they're less likely to follow proper protocols.
3. **Emotional Hijack:** The tone of the message — urgent, demanding, and sometimes intimidating—creates a sense of panic or duty, clouding judgment.

Real-Life Examples

1. **CEO Fraud (Business Email Compromise):** Scammers spoof a CEO's or manager's email address and send urgent requests to employees for money transfers or sensitive information.
2. **Fake Vendor Requests:** A fraudster impersonates a supplier or contractor, claiming overdue payments. They push the victim to act fast to "resolve the issue."
3. **Emergency Text Scams:** A "boss" texts an employee late at night, asking them to make financial transactions on their behalf.

Why It Works

This tactic succeeds because it preys on workplace dynamics. Employees are often reluctant to question authority or delay action, fearing reprimands. Scammers exploit this by mimicking professional communication styles and creating plausible scenarios that feel too urgent to ignore.

How to Spot the Urgent Boss

1. **Inconsistencies in Email or Text Details:** Look for slight discrepancies in email addresses, grammar, or tone that don't match the usual communication style of your boss.
2. **Unusual Requests:** Be cautious if the request involves sensitive information, urgent financial transactions, or tasks outside your typical responsibilities.

3. **No Verification Channels:** Legitimate managers will often provide follow-up options, such as a phone number to confirm. Scammers usually avoid this.

Exercise: Spot the Urgent Spoof

1. Collect examples of emails or messages that ask to be actioned immediately (e.g. "Wire money now," "Respond within 1 hour").
2. Examine:
   - Are the email addresses or phone numbers legitimate?
   - Does the tone feel rushed or overly formal?
3. Write down three signs of urgency-based manipulation you identified.

Role-Playing Drill:

- Partner up and simulate a scenario where one person poses as a boss making an urgent request (e.g. financial transfer or login details).
- Practice verifying the request calmly by asking questions or confirming via a separate channel.

Key Takeaway

The Urgent Boss tactic works by combining authority with time pressure. Stay calm, go through all requests through trusted channels, and don't let urgency override critical thinking.

Chapter 7: The Insider Illusion

The Familiar Face in the Crowd

The **Insider Illusion** is a tactic where social engineers pretend to belong to a group, gaining trust and access by blending in. This could mean posing as a co-worker, contractor, or even a friend of an employee. The goal is simple: exploit the assumption that they are "one of us."

For example:

A man walks into a company office carrying a toolbox and wearing a uniform. He tells the receptionist he's there to repair the server room. Without hesitation, he's let in, despite not being scheduled. In reality, he's a fraudster planting malicious software on the company's systems.

This tactic relies on familiarity and routine. When someone looks or acts the part, people rarely stop to question their presence.

How It Works

1. **Familiarity Bias:** Humans are less likely to question someone who appears to belong to their environment.
2. **Confidence and Routine:** Social engineers often act confidently, exploiting people's tendency to avoid confrontation.
3. **Lack of Verification:** Many workplaces fail to verify identities for routine tasks, assuming everyone present is authorized.

Real-Life Examples

1. **Fake IT Workers:** Imposters pose as IT support, gaining physical or remote access to sensitive systems.
2. **Tailgating:** Someone follows an employee through a secure door by pretending they forgot their ID badge.
3. **Impersonating Co-workers:** Fraudsters claim to be new hires or contractors to gain access to restricted areas or information.

Why It Works

The Insider Illusion thrives in environments where trust and familiarity are prioritized over strict security protocols. It also preys on the human tendency to avoid awkward situations, such as questioning someone who seems to belong.

How to Spot the Insider Illusion

1. **Unscheduled Appearances:** Be alert to people showing up unexpectedly, especially if they claim to be new hires or contractors.
2. **Avoiding Specifics:** Imposters often provide vague answers when questioned about their purpose or role.
3. **Relying on Bystanders' Politeness:** Watch for individuals who tailgate through secure doors or rely on others to hold the door open.

Exercise: Identify Weak Access Points

1. Walk through your home, office, or shared space.
2. Note any potential vulnerabilities where someone could gain unauthorized access (e.g. unsecured doors, lack of ID checks).
3. Write down two simple solutions to improve security, like enforcing badge checks or questioning unfamiliar faces.

Role-Playing Drill:

- Role-play with a partner: One acts as an imposter insider (e.g. a "new hire" or "contractor"), while the other verifies their credentials.
- Use polite questions like:
  - "Who requested your visit?"
  - "May I confirm this with your supervisor?"
- Swap roles and discuss the responses.

Key Takeaway

The Insider Illusion exploits routine and trust. Always suss out unfamiliar people, especially those who appear confident or claim to belong — your caution is a security asset.

Chapter 8: The Overconfidence Play

The Power of Confidence

Imagine you're standing near the entrance of a secured building, and someone confidently strides in without hesitation. They nod politely, say, "Morning," and keep walking. Do you stop them? Probably not. They act like they belong, so you assume they do.

This is the **Overconfidence Play**, a social engineering tactic where manipulators use boldness, assertiveness, and swagger to lower suspicion. By projecting certainty, they exploit human reluctance to challenge others — especially those who appear sure of themselves.

Confidence is persuasive. Humans naturally trust people who act decisively. Combine that with the discomfort of confrontation, and the Overconfidence Play becomes an effective tool for gaining unauthorized access, extracting information, or manipulating decisions.

How It Works

The Overconfidence Play relies on three key elements:

1. **Body Language and Tone:** Manipulators maintain steady eye contact, use strong posture, and speak with authority, making others hesitant to question them.
2. **Assumed Authority:** They use confidence to project authority, acting as though they are in control of the situation.
3. **Social Discomfort:** Most people avoid awkward or confrontational situations. Manipulators leverage this to their advantage, relying on others' desire to "not cause trouble."

Real-Life Examples

1. **Physical Access:** A fraudster confidently enters a secure office, walking through doors held open by employees too polite to stop them.
2. **Fake Deliveries:** Someone drops off packages at an office, acting as though it's routine, while covertly planting surveillance devices or stealing information.
3. **Verbal Authority:** A scammer confidently calls a business, demanding immediate access to files or systems, stating, "I'm the IT manager — just do it."

Why It Works

Confidence overrides doubt. People are less likely to challenge someone who projects authority because it feels awkward or risky to question them. The Overconfidence Play exploits two psychological principles:

- **The Authority Bias:** Confidence often mimics authority, making people comply without verifying legitimacy.
- **Avoidance of Conflict:** Most people prefer to avoid confrontations, especially with someone who seems certain and assertive.

How to Spot the Overconfidence Play

1. **Unverified Assumptions:** Be cautious when someone acts like they belong but offers no credentials or context.
2. **Pressured Compliance:** Manipulators often expect you to comply immediately without giving you time to think or question.
3. **Vague Details:** Confident manipulators avoid specifics when questioned, often dismissing concerns with phrases like, "It's standard procedure."

Exercise: Challenge Assumed Confidence

1. Observe a public setting (e.g. office, café, or event). Watch how confident individuals gain trust without providing credentials.
2. Note three instances where confidence seemed to bypass scrutiny. Reflect on how you would challenge such behavior respectfully.

Role-Playing Drill:

- Partner with someone and take turns acting as the "confident intruder." One person pretends to enter a restricted area or request sensitive information assertively.
- Practice politely challenging them:
    - "I need to confirm who you're here to see."
    - "May I see your identification?"

Key Takeaway

The Overconfidence Play works because boldness suppresses suspicion. Don't let confidence alone determine trust. Ask for verification, even if it feels uncomfortable.

Chapter 9: The Trust Triangle

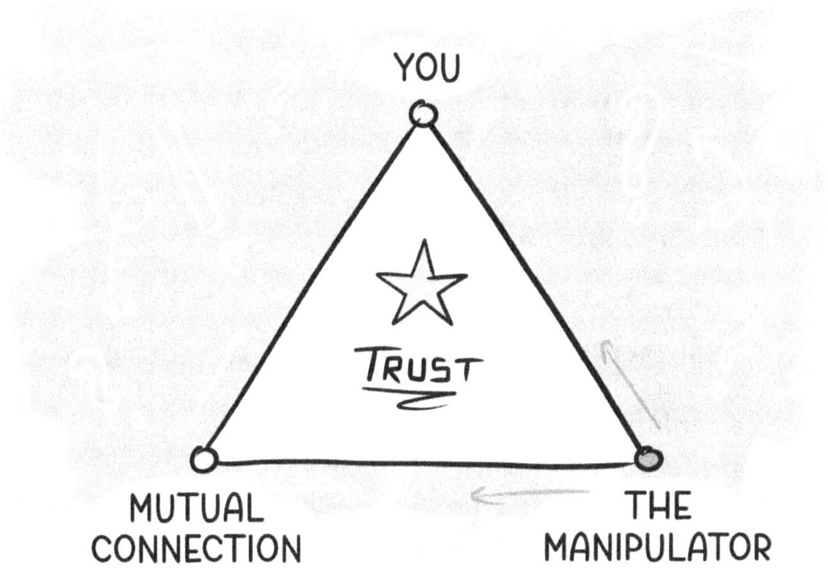

Trust by Association

The **Trust Triangle** tactic is based on a simple principle: trust can spread. When someone claims to know a mutual friend, colleague, or organization, you're more likely to trust them too. This association builds an invisible bridge, encouraging cooperation.

Here's an example:

You get a call from a "vendor" who says, "I've worked with your colleague Sarah on this project before. She gave me your number to finalize the details." Because Sarah's name is familiar, you assume the person is legitimate. Without hesitation, you provide the information they request.

In reality, the manipulator doesn't know Sarah. They've simply dropped her name to gain your trust.

How It Works

The Trust Triangle exploits relationships and social connections through three steps:

1. **Identifying a Mutual Connection:** Manipulators gather information about people you know or organizations you trust.
2. **Name-Dropping:** They casually mention the connection to build credibility and seem familiar.
3. **Leaning on Trust:** By linking themselves to someone you trust, they try to build trust.

Real-Life Examples

1. **The Fake Vendor:** "I worked with your manager last week, and they mentioned you're the one to help me with this request."
2. **Social Media Exploit:** Scammers use mutual friends or colleagues on LinkedIn to gain trust before sending fraudulent messages.
3. **Family or Friend Connection:** "Your cousin recommended me for this service — I've done work for them before."

Why It Works

Humans are social creatures. When someone references a trusted connection, it triggers **associative trust**, making them seem credible by default. The brain takes a shortcut: "If I trust Sarah, and Sarah trusts them, they must be safe."

How to Spot the Trust Triangle

1. **Unverified References:** Be cautious of vague mentions of mutual contacts. Ask for details that confirm the connection.
2. **Overreliance on Trust:** Manipulators lean on the name-drop without offering other evidence of legitimacy.
3. **Contextual Inconsistencies:** If something feels off, check in with the mutual connection directly before proceeding.

Exercise: Establish Connections

1. Write down three recent instances where someone mentioned a mutual contact to gain your trust.

2. Reflect: Did you verify the connection? If not, consider how you could have confirmed their legitimacy without offending them.

Role-Playing Drill:

- Partner with a friend. One person pretends to gain trust by referencing a mutual contact. The other practices validating the connection by asking specific follow-up questions:
    - "What did you and Sarah work on together?"
    - "Let me quickly check with Sarah before moving forward."

Key Takeaway

The Trust Triangle works by exploiting your connections. Always check mutual references — trust should be earned, not borrowed through association.

Chapter 10: The Chain of Command

Manipulating the Chain of Command

You receive an urgent email from your manager asking you to "approve a wire transfer immediately" to resolve a critical vendor issue. Without hesitation, you comply—it's coming from your manager, after all. Later, you discover that your manager's account was hacked, and the transfer was part of a scam.

This is the **Chain of Command** tactic, where manipulators exploit hierarchies to pressure individuals into compliance. By pretending to be a superior or invoking a superior's authority, social engineers override doubt, making targets feel they must obey without question.

How It Works

1. **Impersonating Authority:** The manipulator pretends to be someone higher in the organizational hierarchy, like a manager or executive.

2. **Passing Instructions:** They issue directives through email, phone, or intermediaries, making the request feel routine or mandatory.
3. **Diffuse Responsibility:** Each level of the chain assumes the request has been vetted by someone above, leading to blind compliance.

The Chain of Command works because people in hierarchies are conditioned to follow instructions from superiors, especially in fast-paced or high-pressure environments.

Real-Life Examples

1. **CEO Fraud:** A scammer impersonates a CEO, directing employees to transfer money or share sensitive information.
2. **Bogus Internal Requests:** Fraudsters pretend to be team leads or department heads, asking subordinates for login credentials or system access.
3. **Multi-Level Scams:** Manipulators use a chain of employees to relay fraudulent instructions, ensuring no single person questions the request.

Why It Works

This tactic exploits three key dynamics:

1. **Authority Bias:** People instinctively trust and obey higher-ups in a hierarchy.
2. **Diffusion of Responsibility:** Each link in the chain assumes someone else has verified the legitimacy of the request.
3. **Urgency Over Verification:** Hierarchical directives often come with time pressure, discouraging critical thinking or second-guessing.

How to Spot the Chain of Command

1. **Unusual Requests:** Be wary of directives that seem out of character or fall outside standard procedures.
2. **Lack of Direct Contact:** If the person issuing the directive isn't available to confirm, escalate the situation for verification.

3. **Time Pressure:** Legitimate managers rarely discourage verification, even during urgent tasks.

Exercise: Break the Chain

1. Write down three ways to confirm hierarchical instructions (e.g. "Confirm directly with the source," "Cross-check with a peer," "Follow established escalation protocols").
2. Reflect on a time when you followed a directive without verifying. What questions could you have asked?

Role-Playing Drill:

- One partner plays a "manager" issuing an urgent directive. The other practices checking legitimacy by asking clarifying questions like:
  - "Can I confirm this request with your assistant?"
  - "What's the purpose and urgency of this task?"

Key Takeaway

The Chain of Command leverages organizational structures to manipulate individuals. Always question unusual directives, even if they appear to come from someone higher up.

Chapter 11: The Name Drop

Trust Through Familiarity

"Sarah from Marketing said I should call you. She told me you're the expert on handling client files."

Hearing a familiar name instantly lowers your guard. You trust Sarah, so you extend that trust to the stranger who claims to know her. This is the **Name Drop** tactic — a method social engineers use to fake legitimacy by referencing people or organizations you know.

By strategically mentioning names, roles, or departments, manipulators make themselves appear connected and trustworthy. This false familiarity tricks you into compliance without verification.

How It Works

The Name Drop tactic involves:

1. **Research:** Manipulators gather details about your network—names of co-workers, friends, vendors, or family—often from social media or company directories.

2. **Strategic Mention:** They casually reference a trusted person ("John said you could help me") to build instant credibility.
3. **Assumed Familiarity:** You assume the connection is real and feel socially pressured to cooperate or assist.

Real-Life Examples

1. **Business Scams:** A fraudster emails saying, "Your CEO, Mark, mentioned you'd handle this payment."
2. **Phone Manipulation:** A scammer calls and says, "I was just on the phone with Emily from IT. She asked me to finish this with you."
3. **Social Scams:** Someone messages you on social media, claiming, "I'm a friend of Mike's—he said you're reliable and could help me."

Why It Works

Humans instinctively trust connections. When someone mentions a familiar name, your brain associates them with that person's credibility. This creates a shortcut: "If they know someone I trust, they must be trustworthy too."

The Name Drop also leverages **social pressure** — it feels awkward to question someone who "knows your friend."

How to Spot the Name Drop

1. **Casual References:** Be cautious when someone references a person or organization without providing specifics.
2. **Missing Context:** If the connection feels vague, ask for more details ("When did you last speak to Sarah?").
3. **Verify Directly:** Confirm the claim with the referenced person before proceeding.

Exercise: Establish Whether A Connection Is True

1. Think of three instances where someone referenced a mutual contact to gain your trust.
2. Reflect on whether you verified the claim. Write down one question you could ask next time, like, "Can you tell me how you know them?"

Role-Playing Drill:

- Partner up. One person acts as the manipulator using a name drop: "John said I should talk to you."
- The other practices checking the connection without hesitation: "Let me quickly check with John to confirm."

Key Takeaway

The Name Drop exploits your trust in mutual connections. Never accept references at face value — don't let familiarity override caution.

Chapter 12: The Call from the Top

Manipulating with Authority

You receive a call: "This is the CEO. We're finalizing a critical deal, and I need you to wire funds immediately." The voice is authoritative, the situation urgent. You comply, wanting to avoid delays or questions. Later, you realize the caller wasn't the CEO—it was a scammer impersonating them.

This is the **Call from the Top** tactic, where fraudsters use fake authority to force compliance. By pretending to be senior leadership, manipulators create pressure, fear, and urgency to override logical decision-making.

How It Works

1. **Assuming Authority:** The scammer uses names, roles, or insider details to sound convincing as a high-level executive.

2. **Creating Pressure:** They frame the request as critical and time-sensitive, making verification seem unnecessary or risky.
3. **Avoiding Scrutiny:** Fraudsters rely on the target's reluctance to question leadership or delay urgent tasks.

Real-Life Examples

1. **CEO Impersonation:** Fraudsters impersonate executives, demanding urgent wire transfers to close "important deals."
2. **Fake Vendor Approvals:** Scammers claim to represent leadership, authorizing fraudulent payments or access to systems.
3. **Emergency Directives:** A manipulator pretends to be a CEO handling a crisis, using fear to push compliance.

Why It Works

The Call from the Top preys on two dynamics:

1. **Authority Bias:** People instinctively follow instructions from perceived superiors.
2. **Fear of Repercussions:** Employees fear delaying or challenging executive requests, leading to blind compliance.

How to Spot the Call from the Top

1. **Unusual Communication:** Executives rarely contact subordinates directly for sensitive or urgent tasks.
2. **Time-Sensitive Demands:** Verify any request that discourages verification or asks for immediate action.
3. **Out-of-Character Requests:** If the task feels uncharacteristic of the sender, confirm through official channels.

Exercise: Prove Executive Directives

1. Write down three steps to confirm high-level requests (e.g. "Call the executive's office," "Check with a trusted colleague," "Request written confirmation").
2. Practice applying these steps to a simulated executive directive with a partner.

Role-Playing Drill:

- One person plays the "executive" issuing an urgent request. The other practices making sure of facts calmly, saying:
  - "I'd like to confirm this with your assistant."
  - "Can you send this request through official channels?"

Key Takeaway

The Call from the Top uses authority and urgency to manipulate decisions. Always verify executive requests, and remember: true leadership welcomes questions.

Chapter 13: The Financial Fraudster

The Credible Payment Request

You receive an email, phone call, or invoice from what seems like a trusted vendor, supplier, or even an internal team member: "Payment overdue — please send the outstanding amount to this account immediately." Everything looks legitimate — logos, formatting, and tone — so you process the payment. A week later, you discover the vendor never requested it. The money? Gone.

The **Financial Fraudster** exploits trust in financial processes to steal money or sensitive payment information. By mimicking legitimate payment systems, impersonating trusted vendors, or posing as internal finance teams, social engineers manipulate employees into approving fraudulent transactions.

How It Works

This tactic relies on financial familiarity and trust:

1. **Mimicking Legitimacy:** Fraudsters create realistic invoices, emails, or requests that mirror those from trusted vendors or colleagues.
2. **Exploiting Routine:** In busy workplaces, financial processes like invoice payments are often repetitive and rushed. Scammers exploit this by inserting fraudulent requests into the workflow.
3. **Urgency and Consequences:** Phrases like "overdue," "penalties," or "service interruptions" pressure targets into acting quickly.

Real-Life Examples

1. **Vendor Invoice Fraud:** A scammer impersonates a supplier, sending fake invoices to companies that look identical to the real ones.
2. **Account Switch Requests:** Fraudsters contact finance teams claiming the vendor's bank account details have "changed" and provide new payment information.
3. **Internal Finance Impersonation:** An email from "accounts payable" demands a quick wire transfer to resolve an "urgent payment error."

Why It Works

The Financial Fraudster preys on trust, routine, and urgency. Financial processes often involve multiple parties, making it easier to insert fraudulent steps unnoticed. Employees assume payment requests are legitimate if they:

- Look official (correct logos, formatting).
- Reference real projects, departments, or deadlines.
- Appear urgent and linked to potential penalties.

How to Spot the Financial Fraudster

1. **Unusual Changes:** Be cautious of last-minute requests to change payment details or bank accounts.
2. **Mismatched Details:** Check email addresses, account numbers, and invoice references. Subtle discrepancies often signal fraud.

3. **Urgent Financial Demands:** Legitimate vendors rarely ask for instant payments under threat of severe penalties.

Exercise: Payment Verification Drill

1. Review the last five financial payment requests you processed. Write down the steps you followed to confirm legitimacy.
2. Next time, add an extra verification step, such as confirming payment details via a phone call to a known contact.

Role-Playing Drill:

- Partner up. One person acts as the "fraudster," submitting a fake invoice or urgent payment request.
- The other practices spotting red flags and challenging the request:
  - "I'll confirm the account details with the vendor directly."

Key Takeaway

The Financial Fraudster exploits routine financial processes with fake urgency. Always verify payment requests, especially changes to account details — legitimacy is proven, not assumed.

Chapter 14: The Benevolent Guide

The Trap of Misplaced Help

You're lost at a conference, struggling to find a specific room when someone approaches. They smile warmly and say, "You look lost. I know where that room is — follow me." Relieved, you follow. Along the way, they ask questions about your role, team, or work. Harmless? Not really. You've just shared information with someone whose motives aren't as "helpful" as they seemed.

This is the **Benevolent Guide**—a tactic where manipulators use friendliness and helpfulness to gain trust. Unlike more aggressive approaches, this strategy exploits human goodwill, using a false sense of support to access information, systems, or spaces.

Social engineers know that when someone seems helpful, we're less likely to question their intentions. After all, who distrusts a good Samaritan?

How It Works

1. **Offering Assistance:** The manipulator approaches you, often at a moment of confusion, frustration, or need, offering to "help."
2. **Building Rapport:** They create trust through small talk, shared experiences, or casual questions to lower your defenses.
3. **Gaining Access or Information:** Under the guise of helping, they extract details, gain entry to restricted spaces, or establish themselves as "familiar" for future manipulations.

This strategy thrives in busy environments where people may feel rushed, stressed, or unfamiliar with their surroundings — offices, airports, events, or online platforms.

Real-Life Examples

1. **Event Impersonators:** At conferences, a scammer offers to "show you the way" but subtly probes for job details, credentials, or access.
2. **Online Helpers:** Someone in a chatroom or on social media offers to "guide" you through a problem (e.g., tech issues), tricking you into revealing passwords or installing malicious software.
3. **Fake Employees:** A friendly "colleague" helps a new employee access systems, convincing them to share logins or ignore security protocols.

Why It Works

Humans instinctively respond positively to kindness. This manipulation relies on three key factors:

1. **Goodwill Bias:** People feel grateful when someone helps them and are reluctant to question their motives.
2. **Lowered Defenses:** In moments of need or confusion, critical thinking is often replaced with relief and trust.
3. **Social Pressure:** Rejecting help can feel rude or ungrateful, leading victims to comply even when they're unsure.

How to Spot the Benevolent Guide

1. **Unsolicited Help:** Be cautious of strangers who offer help before you've asked for it — especially if they start probing for information.
2. **Overfriendly Behavior:** Manipulators often overextend friendliness to create quick trust.
3. **Subtle Questions:** Look out for small, probing questions about your role, team, or systems that seem unrelated to the help being offered.

Exercise: Recognize Unsolicited Help

1. Think of a time when someone offered unsolicited help. Did they ask questions that seemed unusual or unrelated? Write down two ways you could politely decline next time.

Role-Playing Drill:

- Partner up. One person plays the "benevolent guide" offering unsolicited help while subtly extracting details (e.g. "What's your role again?" or "Oh, so that's your login setup?").
- The other practices politely deflecting and verifying the person's legitimacy:
    - "Thank you, but I'll figure this out myself."
    - "What team are you with? Let me confirm this with my manager."

Key Takeaway

The Benevolent Guide manipulates trust under the guise of kindness. Stay polite but cautious of helpful offers, especially when they come unsolicited or lead to sharing information.

Chapter 15: The Legal Threat

Fear of the Law as a Weapon

You open your inbox to find a stern-looking email: **"Legal Notice: Immediate Payment Required to Avoid Lawsuit."** The message claims you've violated a copyright, owe unpaid taxes, or need to pay a fine to avoid prosecution. Panic sets in. To avoid trouble, you comply immediately.

This is the **Legal Threat** tactic where manipulators use fabricated legal claims to scare victims into quick action. Whether it's through fake fines, lawsuits, or "official warnings," the goal is to exploit fear and authority to coerce compliance.

How It Works

1. **Fabricated Claims:** Manipulators create false accusations (e.g. unpaid debts, copyright violations) to create panic.
2. **Official Tone and Language:** They use formal wording, fake legal jargon, and "official-looking" documents to appear credible.

3. **Immediate Consequences:** They emphasize urgency with threats of lawsuits, financial penalties, or even jail time to pressure victims into action.

This tactic is effective because few people want to challenge "legal" claims. They fear embarrassment, reputational damage, or financial harm.

Real-Life Examples

1. **Fake Copyright Notices:** Scammers send emails claiming you've used copyrighted content illegally and need to pay a fine.
2. **Tax Scams:** Fraudsters impersonate tax authorities, threatening penalties or arrests for "unpaid taxes."
3. **Debt Collection Fraud:** A fake legal firm claims you owe money and demands immediate payment to avoid a court case.

Why It Works

The Legal Threat manipulates three key emotions:

1. **Fear of Authority:** Legal consequences feel serious, and most people comply to avoid confrontation.
2. **Panic-Induced Compliance:** Urgent legal threats trigger quick, irrational decisions.
3. **Lack of Legal Knowledge:** Many people are unfamiliar with legal processes and assume the threat is real.

How to Spot the Legal Threat

1. **Unverified Sources:** Check the sender's email, phone number, or credentials. Official agencies rarely threaten action via email or phone.
2. **Urgent Tone:** Real legal warnings follow processes and timelines — scammers rush you into acting immediately.
3. **Unclear Details:** Fake legal claims often lack specifics, like case numbers or contact information for verification.

Exercise: Verify Legal Claims

1. Write down three steps to check any legal or financial claim (e.g. "Check the sender's official website, call the agency directly, and request written confirmation").

2. Practice applying these steps to a suspicious email or letter example.

Role-Playing Drill:

- Partner up. One person acts as the "legal threat," using vague claims or intimidating wording to pressure payment.
- The other practices staying calm and verifying the legitimacy:
    - "Please send me an official case reference so I can confirm with the agency."

Key Takeaway

The Legal Threat tactic relies on fear and intimidation. Stay calm, check claims through legitimate sources, and never let panic dictate your actions.

Chapter 16: The Medical Manipulator

Exploiting Health and Fear

Imagine receiving a call from someone claiming to be your doctor's office: "We noticed an issue with your recent medical test results. To resolve it, we need to confirm your personal details and insurance information." Concerned and eager to resolve the problem, you comply without hesitation. Hours later, you realize the call was a scam.

This is the **Medical Manipulator** tactic. Scammers impersonate medical professionals, healthcare organizations, or insurance providers to exploit your trust in the medical system. They use fear, urgency, or confusion about health to extract sensitive information, financial details, or even payments.

Health-related issues are personal and often stressful, which makes people particularly vulnerable to manipulation in this context.

How It Works

1. **Impersonation of Trustworthy Figures:** Scammers pose as doctors, medical staff, or health insurance agents to create legitimacy.
2. **Urgency and Fear:** They use phrases like "urgent test results," "insurance lapsing," or "unresolved medical bills" to incite fear and pressure victims into action.
3. **Request for Sensitive Information:** The manipulator asks for personal details such as Social Security numbers, medical records, payment information, or insurance credentials.

This tactic is particularly dangerous because health-related concerns often push people to comply out of fear for their well-being or finances.

Real-Life Examples

1. **Fake Test Results:** A scammer calls claiming there's a serious issue with your medical tests, asking for your date of birth, Social Security number, and payment to "resolve" the issue.
2. **Health Insurance Scams:** Fraudsters impersonate insurance providers, warning that your policy is expiring and demanding immediate payment to "reinstate" it.
3. **Medical Billing Fraud:** Someone posing as a hospital billing representative claims you owe money for a recent procedure and pressures you to pay immediately over the phone.

Why It Works

The Medical Manipulator tactic preys on three critical vulnerabilities:

1. **Fear for Health:** Health is deeply personal, and the fear of something being "wrong" overrides doubt.
2. **Trust in Medical Professionals:** Doctors and medical staff are trusted authority figures, so their requests rarely get questioned.
3. **Urgency in Health Matters:** Medical concerns often feel time-sensitive, leading people to act without confirming legitimacy.

Scammers take advantage of these emotions to manipulate victims into compliance.

How to Spot the Medical Manipulator

1. **Unsolicited Calls or Emails:** Be wary of unexpected messages about medical test results, bills, or insurance. Legitimate providers rarely reach out this way.
2. **Requests for Sensitive Details:** Genuine medical institutions already have your information and won't ask for Social Security numbers or payment details over the phone.
3. **Pressure to Act Immediately:** Scammers emphasize urgency, using fear tactics like "fines" or "cancellation of treatment" to discourage verification.

Exercise: Verify Medical Requests

1. Write down three questions to ask anyone who calls claiming to be from a medical office:
    - "What is your full name and position?"
    - "Can I call your office directly to confirm this?"
    - "What's the reference number for my case?"
2. Practice responding calmly to a fake "urgent" call scenario with a friend.

Self-Awareness Drill:

- Reflect on a time when you acted quickly out of fear or urgency regarding health or medical issues. Write down steps you can take next time before acting, such as contacting your doctor's office directly.

Key Takeaway

The Medical Manipulator tactic uses fear and trust to exploit your health concerns. Stay calm, verify requests directly with your healthcare provider, and never share sensitive information over unsolicited calls or emails.

Chapter 17: The Social Media Savior

The Illusion of Help Online

You're scrolling through social media when you notice a comment or message offering help: "Having trouble with your account? I can fix that for you—just send me your login details!" Grateful for the "assistance," you comply, only to realize later that your account has been hacked.

The **Social Media Savior** tactic is a method where scammers pose as helpful individuals or customer support representatives online. They exploit the trust and familiarity of social platforms to trick you into sharing sensitive information, granting access to accounts, or clicking malicious links.

In a digital world where problems arise daily — forgotten passwords, hacked accounts, or fake giveaways — this tactic preys on the desire for quick solutions.

How It Works

1. **Impersonating Help:** Scammers pose as official customer support, friends, or "tech-savvy" individuals offering help.
2. **Building Trust:** They message you directly, often using polite and friendly language to make you feel comfortable.
3. **Gaining Information or Access:** Under the guise of fixing a problem, they ask for login credentials, reset codes, or direct access to your device.

Real-Life Examples

1. **Fake Customer Support:** A scammer comments on your post about a locked social media account, claiming they can help—if you share your reset code.
2. **The "Helpful Friend":** Someone messages you, claiming they noticed suspicious activity on your account and offers to "fix" it.
3. **Malicious Links:** A "support representative" sends a link to a fake recovery site that steals your login details when entered.

Why It Works

The Social Media Savior manipulates two key emotions:

1. **Relief in Crisis:** When facing account problems, people seek quick solutions, making them vulnerable to fake helpers.
2. **Trust in Familiar Platforms:** Social media feels safe, and people rarely question the legitimacy of "helpful" comments or messages.

The scam works because it blends in — appearing supportive, trustworthy, and timely.

How to Spot the Social Media Savior

1. **Unsolicited Offers of Help:** Be wary of messages or comments offering assistance you didn't request.
2. **Requests for Login or Reset Codes:** Legitimate support teams never ask for passwords or reset information.

3. **Suspicious Links:** Hover over any link before clicking to confirm its authenticity.

Exercise: Spot the Fake Helper

1. Scroll through comments or messages on a social media platform. Look for examples of unsolicited "help" (e.g. fake customer support).
2. Write down three red flags you notice, such as vague profiles, suspicious links, or urgent requests for credentials.

Practice Response Drill:

- With a partner, role-play a scenario where one person poses as a "fake helper" offering to fix an account issue.
- The other practices responding:
  - "Thank you, but I'll contact the company directly through their official support page."

Key Takeaway

The Social Media Savior exploits your trust and urgency online. Always verify support requests through official channels and never share credentials or reset codes with anyone.

Chapter 18: The Customer Service Con

The Illusion of Professional Help

You receive a call or message: **“This is customer support. We’ve detected an issue with your account.”** The voice is calm, professional, and reassuring. They walk you through "fixing" the problem — asking for passwords, login codes, or payment details to “verify your identity.” Trusting the person, you comply, only to realize your account is now compromised.

This is the **Customer Service Con**, a tactic where scammers impersonate legitimate support teams to exploit trust and extract sensitive information. Whether it’s for banks, streaming services, or e-commerce sites, these fraudsters capitalize on the assumption that customer service exists to help — not harm.

The scam thrives on two factors: the impersonator’s professional demeanor and the target’s urgency to resolve the issue quickly.

How It Works

1. **Professional Presentation:** Scammers use polished scripts, professional language, and fake call center environments to appear credible.
2. **Fake Problems:** They invent issues like suspicious account activity, billing failures, or subscription cancellations to create panic and urgency.
3. **Data Harvesting:** Under the pretense of "solving" the problem, they request sensitive details, such as passwords, PINs, card numbers, or multi-factor authentication codes.

Whether over the phone, email, or chat, their strategy is to seem so helpful and professional that you don't think twice about letting your guard down.

Real-Life Examples

1. **Bank Fraud Calls:** A scammer posing as your bank's support team calls about "suspicious withdrawals," asking you to confirm your account details.
2. **The Support Agent Scams:** You receive an unsolicited call claiming your computer has a virus. The "support agent" requests remote access to "fix it," but instead steals files.
3. **Subscription Scams:** A fake email claims your Netflix or Amazon subscription has been canceled due to payment failure, prompting you to "log in" through a malicious link.

Why It Works

The **Customer Service Con** exploits key psychological tendencies:

1. **Trust in Professionalism:** People instinctively trust calm, polite, and knowledgeable voices that resemble legitimate customer support.
2. **Urgency and Panic:** By creating fake problems, scammers push victims to act rather than question authenticity.

3. **Desire for Resolution:** When you hear there's an issue with your account, the immediate goal is to resolve it—not check the legitimacy of the source.

The more professional the impersonator seems, the more difficult it becomes to doubt them.

How to Spot the Customer Service Con

1. **Unsolicited Contact:** Legitimate companies rarely call or email you about issues you haven't reported yourself. Be wary of unexpected support outreach.
2. **Requests for Sensitive Details:** Real customer service teams never ask for passwords, PINs, or verification codes.
3. **High-Pressure Solutions:** Scammers often push for quick action, like clicking links or granting remote access to your devices.

Exercise: Test Customer Support Legitimacy

1. Write down two steps to verify a customer service request (e.g. "Call the official company support line" or "Check the company's website for ongoing issues").
2. Practice these steps with a partner simulating a fake support call asking for sensitive details.

Scenario Drill:

- Imagine receiving a call from "your bank's support team." Practice responding with verification steps like:
    - "Can I call you back through the official number on my card?"
    - "I'll log in through the official website instead of sharing details over the phone."

Key Takeaway

The Customer Service Con works by mimicking professionalism and urgency. Always check support claims directly through official service providers, and never share sensitive information during unsolicited calls or emails.

Chapter 19: The Policeman's Bluff

The Power of Intimidation

You receive a call: **"This is Officer Smith from your local police department. There's a warrant for your arrest due to unpaid fines. If you settle it now, we can avoid further action."** The voice is stern and authoritative, leaving you rattled. To avoid trouble, you comply — sending money or sharing personal details — only to later discover it was a scam.

This is the **Policeman's Bluff**, a tactic where scammers impersonate law enforcement or legal authorities to intimidate victims into compliance. They rely on fear, authority, and urgency to force quick action to avoid imagined consequences.

How It Works

1. **Authority Mimicry:** Scammers pretend to be police officers, government agents, or court officials, using formal language and intimidating tones.
2. **Threats and Consequences:** They invent urgent scenarios like unpaid fines, missed jury duty, or outstanding warrants to create panic.

3. **Immediate Payment Requests:** To "resolve" the issue, they ask for payment through wire transfers, or bank information.

This tactic works because most people fear legal trouble and feel pressured to comply when they believe an authority figure is involved.

Real-Life Examples

1. **Fake Arrest Warrants:** A scammer claims you have a warrant for unpaid traffic tickets and demands immediate payment to avoid arrest.
2. **IRS or Tax Fraud Calls:** Someone impersonating a government agent claims you owe back taxes, threatening legal action if you don't comply.
3. **Jury Duty Scams:** Fraudsters accuse victims of missing jury duty and request fines to avoid "legal penalties."

Why It Works

The Policeman's Bluff relies on three primary triggers:

1. **Authority Bias:** People are conditioned to respect and obey law enforcement without question.
2. **Fear of Consequences:** The threat of arrest, fines, or legal trouble creates panic and short-circuits logical thinking.
3. **Sense of Urgency:** Scammers emphasize immediate action to prevent victims from verifying their claims.

The fear of "getting in trouble" makes victims comply quickly to resolve the situation.

How to Spot the Policeman's Bluff

1. **Unusual Payment Requests:** Law enforcement agencies will never ask for payment through gift cards, wire transfers, or online links.
2. **Threats of Immediate Arrest:** Real authorities follow legal processes and timelines—not phone calls threatening instant action.
3. **Unverifiable Details:** Scammers often provide vague case numbers or refuse to let you confirm their claims with an official office.

Exercise: Verify Authority Claims

1. Write down three legitimate steps to verify contact from law enforcement (e.g. "Call your local police station directly" or "Request written documentation").
2. Practice applying these steps when presented with a fake scenario of a police or government call.

Role-Playing Drill:

- Partner with a friend. One person acts as the "fake officer" demanding payment.
- Practice staying calm and responding with verification steps:
    - "I'll contact my local police station to confirm this."
    - "Please send me a written notice to verify your claim."

Key Takeaway

The Policeman's Bluff exploits fear of authority to force compliance. Stay calm, verify any legal threats with official channels, and never send payments to resolve a claim you haven't confirmed.

Chapter 20: The Religious Mask

Exploiting Faith and Trust

Imagine someone approaches you outside a place of worship, asking for a donation for "the children's charity run by your local church." They seem devout, humble, and sincere. You hand over money without question, only to find out later that no such charity exists.

This is the **Religious Mask**, a tactic where scammers exploit faith, spirituality, or shared religious values to gain trust and manipulate individuals. By disguising themselves as fellow believers or representatives of religious causes, they tap into emotions such as compassion, trust, and generosity.

Religious institutions and charitable causes hold a sacred space in people's hearts. When someone speaks the "language of faith," people often lower their defenses, assuming sincerity. Social engineers exploit this trust to steal money, gain influence, or extract personal information.

How It Works

1. **Emotional Appeal:** Scammers use religious language, symbols, or affiliations to build trust quickly. They speak of noble causes, divine blessings, or urgent needs to gain sympathy.
2. **Shared Identity:** Manipulators position themselves as part of the same faith or community, creating an instant bond.
3. **Urgency and Guilt:** They emphasize the immediate "need for action" while suggesting that refusing to help is against one's faith or values.

The Religious Mask is especially effective during moments of vulnerability — after tragedies, during holidays, or in places where faith is deeply rooted.

Real-Life Examples

1. **Fake Charity Donations:** Scammers solicit donations for fake religious charities, often with fabricated stories of orphans, disaster relief, or community projects.
2. **Spiritual Manipulation:** A fraudster claims they can "bless" or "pray for" someone's problems—for a fee or in exchange for sensitive information.
3. **Impersonating Religious Leaders:** Scammers pose as trusted clergy members via phone, email, or social media, asking for money or personal information to help "someone in need."

Why It Works

The Religious Mask preys on three powerful emotional triggers:

1. **Trust in Shared Faith:** People instinctively trust those who seem to share their spiritual beliefs or values.
2. **Emotional Appeal:** Religion emphasizes compassion, charity, and helping others, making believers susceptible to manipulation through guilt or goodwill.
3. **Authority in Faith:** Fraudsters posing as religious leaders carry the perceived moral authority of their role, which few people question.

How to Spot the Religious Mask

1. **Unverified Charities:** If someone asks for a donation, verify the charity through official channels or websites before giving.
2. **Pressure to Give Immediately:** Genuine charities rarely request urgent action or suggest guilt for refusing to help.
3. **Unusual Requests from Leaders:** If a religious leader reaches out unexpectedly for money or personal details, confirm directly with them or their organization.

Exercise: Verify Charitable Claims

1. Write down two trusted ways to confirm a charity's legitimacy (e.g., searching official charity registries or contacting your place of worship).
2. Find three examples of religious charity scams online. Identify what red flags you notice, like lack of contact details or unverifiable claims.

Role-Playing Drill:

- Partner with a friend. One person plays the scammer asking for donations "on behalf of the church."
- The other practices responding:
  - "I'll confirm this with the church office first."
  - "Can you provide me with documentation about this charity?"

Key Takeaway

The Religious Mask exploits faith and compassion to manipulate trust. Verify charitable requests and be cautious when shared beliefs are mentioned — true sincerity welcomes verification.

Section 2: Emotional Manipulation Tactics

Emotions drive human behavior. They fuel decisions, reactions, and trust, often without a second thought. Social engineers know this and use emotions as tools to bypass logic and critical thinking. Whether through fear, guilt, flattery, or sympathy, manipulators exploit feelings to make you act on impulse instead of reason.

Think of emotions as buttons on a control panel. Press the right one — panic, pride, or pity — and a person will follow instructions without questioning why. This section uncovers how emotional triggers are weaponized and teaches you to recognize when someone is pulling your strings.

By the end of this section, you'll be able to pause, analyze, and take control of your emotions before they control you.

Chapter 21: The Fear Trigger

The Power of Panic

You open an email that reads: **"Immediate Action Required! Your account has been compromised. Log in now to secure it."** Your heart races, and panic sets in. Without hesitation, you click the link and enter your credentials. Moments later, you realize the email was fake — and you've just handed over your account to a scammer.

This is the **Fear Trigger**, a tactic where social engineers use panic and anxiety to cloud your judgment. By creating fear — whether it's about security breaches, financial losses, or threats of legal trouble — they force you into making quick, irrational decisions.

Fear short-circuits logical thinking. When people are scared, their priority becomes resolving the immediate "threat," often without stopping to verify its legitimacy.

How It Works

1. **Creating a Threat:** Scammers fabricate scenarios that cause fear, like hacked accounts, stolen data, or unpaid fines.
2. **Pressuring Immediate Action:** They emphasize urgency, warning of severe consequences if you don't act quickly.
3. **Providing a "Solution":** The manipulator offers a fake fix, like clicking a malicious link, calling a fraudulent hotline, or sharing sensitive details to "resolve" the issue.

Real-Life Examples

1. **Fake Security Alerts:** Emails claiming your bank account or social media has been hacked, with a link to "reset your password".
2. **Threatening Phone Calls:** A scammer calls pretending to be from the IRS or a debt collector, threatening arrest if you don't pay immediately.
3. **Pop-Up Warnings:** A fake computer pop-up warns of a virus and instructs you to call a bogus number for assistance — leading to a scammer who steals your data.

Why It Works

The Fear Trigger exploits natural human responses to threats:

1. **Fight or Flight Instinct:** Fear triggers a sense of urgency, overriding rational thought in favor of immediate action.
2. **Avoidance of Consequences:** People take swift action to avoid perceived risks, such as financial loss, data theft, or legal penalties.
3. **Blind Trust in Solutions:** Scammers present themselves as the "fix" to the problem they created, leading victims to comply without verifying.

How to Spot the Fear Trigger

1. **Urgent Warnings:** Be careful of messages or calls that use fear or demand immediate action. Real organizations rarely communicate threats this way.
2. **Unusual Solutions:** Legitimate companies don't require you to click strange links, call unknown numbers, or share sensitive details to resolve issues.
3. **Verify Independently:** Pause and confirm the situation directly with the institution mentioned (e.g., your bank or government agency).

Exercise: Pause and Reflect

1. Write down three steps to take when you receive a panic-inducing message (e.g. "Pause, verify through trusted channels, avoid immediate action").
2. Practice applying these steps to a fake security alert email with a partner.

Self-Awareness Drill:

- Reflect on a time when fear made you do something irrational (e.g. clicking a suspicious email). Write down one question you can ask yourself next time: "Is this real, or am I being manipulated?"

Key Takeaway

The Fear Trigger preys on panic and urgency to override logical thinking. Always pause, verify threats through trusted sources, and never let fear push you into immediate, unverified action.

Chapter 22: The Sympathy Card

When Sympathy Is Used Against You

A stranger approaches you outside a store, appearing disheveled and distressed. “My wallet was stolen,” they say, “and I just need $20 to get home. I swear I’ll pay you back.” Your heart goes out to them, and you hand over the cash. But days later, you realize the story didn’t add up.

This is the **Sympathy Card**, a manipulation tactic where fraudsters use emotional stories of hardship, illness, or loss to exploit your kindness and generosity. Whether it’s online, on the phone, or in person, they aim to provoke your sympathy and lower your defenses.

While genuine hardship exists, manipulators weaponize empathy to gain money, information, or access.

How It Works

1. **Crafting a Sob Story:** Manipulators share emotional, often exaggerated, stories about suffering or need.

2. **Earning Trust Through Vulnerability:** They act open, vulnerable, and sincere, making it harder for you to question their honesty.
3. **Request for Help:** They ask for small but immediate assistance—money, personal details, or a favor that escalates later.

The sympathy card works because it exploits compassion and the human desire to "do good."

Real-Life Examples

1. **Street Scams:** A person claims to be stranded or in crisis, asking for money to get home.
2. **Online Fundraising Scams:** Fraudulent crowdfunding campaigns use fake photos and emotional stories to solicit donations.
3. **Fake Illness Appeals:** Scammers claim they or a loved one are sick, asking for money to cover medical expenses.

Why It Works

The Sympathy Card relies on three psychological triggers:

1. **Empathy and Compassion:** People want to help others in pain or distress, especially when they're made to feel they can "make a difference."
2. **Trust in Vulnerability:** Vulnerable behavior feels honest, so people are less likely to doubt it.
3. **Social Pressure:** Saying "no" to someone suffering feels uncomfortable and unkind, pushing you into compliance.

How to Spot the Sympathy Card

1. **Inconsistent Details:** Emotional stories are often vague or exaggerated—look for details that don't add up.
2. **Immediate Requests:** Be cautious when someone asks for quick assistance without offering ways to verify their story.
3. **Overly Emotional Appeals:** If a request seems designed solely to pull at your heartstrings, pause and assess its legitimacy.

Exercise: Question Emotional Appeals

1. Think of a time someone shared an emotional story to gain your help. Reflect on whether you verified their claim. Write down two ways to check emotional requests, like asking for specifics or suggesting alternative help.

Role-Playing Drill:

- Partner up. One person tells an emotional story to gain assistance. The other practices responding kindly but cautiously:
  - "I'm sorry to hear that. Let me check if there's another way to help."
  - "Can you provide more information so I can confirm your story?"

Key Takeaway

The Sympathy Card manipulates your kindness with emotional stories. Compassion is valuable, but don't let it override caution — verify before you act, and remember that genuine requests can stand up to scrutiny.

Chapter 23: The Guilt Lever

How Guilt Becomes a Weapon

Imagine this: A co-worker comes to you, looking desperate. They say, "If you don't help me with this login, I'll lose my job. Please, my family depends on me." It's not your responsibility, but guilt creeps in. You share the details because you feel obligated. Later, you realize you were manipulated.

This is the **Guilt Lever**, a strategy where social engineers use guilt to force compliance. By framing themselves as victims or implying that your refusal will harm someone, they exploit your desire to do the "right thing" or avoid being seen as unkind.

Humans naturally want to help others and avoid causing harm. Manipulators twist this instinct, using guilt to bypass rational thought and make you act against your better judgment.

How It Works

1. **Playing the Victim:** The manipulator presents themselves as someone struggling, wronged, or in dire need of help.

2. **Creating Emotional Obligation:** They make you feel responsible for their situation, subtly implying that refusing to help makes you a bad person.
3. **Reinforcing Consequences:** They emphasize what might happen if you don't comply — lost jobs, broken relationships, or other dramatic fallout.

The Guilt Lever thrives because humans hate the feeling of letting someone down, even when the guilt is undeserved.

Real-Life Examples

1. **The Colleague in Crisis:** A "co-worker" or stranger claims they need a favor — such as access to files or logins — to avoid catastrophic consequences.
2. **Charity Scams:** Scammers ask for money, telling exaggerated stories about suffering children, families, or animals, leaving you feeling heartless if you decline.
3. **Fake Family Emergencies:** Someone posing as a distant relative messages you, claiming they're in trouble and need money immediately.

Why It Works

The Guilt Lever manipulates three emotional triggers:

1. **Avoiding Shame:** Refusing to help makes you feel selfish, unkind, or uncaring.
2. **Desire to Do Good:** Most people want to help those in need, especially when they're made to feel uniquely able to help.
3. **Fear of Consequences:** By framing the request as urgent and dramatic, manipulators make you feel personally responsible for the fallout.

In these moments, guilt overwhelms logic, making it harder to say no.

How to Spot the Guilt Lever

1. **Excessive Emotional Appeal:** Be wary of stories or pleas that seem exaggerated, overly dramatic, or designed to provoke an emotional response.

2. **Personal Responsibility Claims:** Watch for phrases like, "You're my last hope," or "Without you, I don't know what I'll do."
3. **Immediate Consequences:** If someone uses urgency to pressure you, pause and evaluate the legitimacy of their claim.

Exercise: Recognize Guilt Traps

1. Reflect on a situation where you felt guilty into compliance. Was it justified? Write down three signs you overlooked that the guilt was manipulative.
2. Practice saying "no" to unreasonable emotional requests by responding with:
    - "I'm sorry, but I can't help with that right now."
    - "Let me confirm the situation first."

Role-Playing Drill:

- Partner with someone. One person plays the manipulator, exaggerating a crisis to invoke guilt. The other practices staying calm and saying "no" firmly but kindly.

Key Takeaway

The Guilt Lever manipulates your desire to help others by creating false responsibility. Don't let guilt cloud your logic. Pause, evaluate the situation, and remember that saying "no" doesn't make you unkind.

Chapter 24: The Flattery Trap

How Compliments Turn into Traps

Imagine a stranger emails you: "You're so talented! Your work is exactly what we need for our next big project." They continue to praise your skills and intelligence, offering a "special" opportunity. Flattered, you're eager to say yes. Without realizing it, you've just handed over sensitive details or money for a scam that never existed.

This is the **Flattery Trap**, a tactic where manipulators use excessive praise to gain your trust. Compliments lower defenses by appealing to your ego, making you more likely to comply with requests or ignore red flags.

Flattery isn't inherently bad, but when it's used as a weapon, it clouds judgment and encourages impulsive decisions.

How It Works

1. **Over-the-Top Praise:** Manipulators use exaggerated compliments to make you feel special, admired, or indispensable.

2. **Lowering Defenses:** Flattery feels good. It creates a bond of trust, distracting you from asking critical questions or spotting inconsistencies.
3. **The Favor Request:** Once trust is established, the manipulator leverages your good mood and ego to make a request—whether it's information, access, or money.

The Flattery Trap thrives because humans are naturally drawn to positive reinforcement and validation, especially when it seems to come from credible or influential people.

Real-Life Examples

1. **Phony Job Offers:** Scammers compliment your "unique skills" or "amazing portfolio" to entice you into sharing personal details or paying fees for a fake job opportunity.
2. **Social Media Manipulation:** A stranger praises your photos or posts, eventually steering the conversation to requests for personal information or financial help.
3. **Fake Business Proposals:** Fraudsters flatter professionals with promises of partnerships or contracts, only to extract money or proprietary information.

Why It Works

The Flattery Trap exploits the following emotional triggers:

1. **Ego Boost:** Compliments feel good and create a sense of connection, making you less critical of the person's intentions.
2. **Desire for Recognition:** People crave validation, especially for their talents, work, or personality. Flattery fulfills this need.
3. **Reciprocity Effect:** Praise creates a subtle sense of obligation, making you more likely to "return the favor" by complying with requests.

When someone praises you, it feels awkward to question or reject them. Manipulators know this and use it to their advantage.

How to Spot the Flattery Trap

1. **Excessive Praise:** Genuine compliments are specific and balanced. Be wary of flattery that feels too over-the-top.
2. **Rapid Trust-Building:** If compliments are quickly followed by requests for favors, money, or access, pause and evaluate their intentions.
3. **Unfamiliar Sources:** Compliments from strangers or people you've never interacted with often signal manipulation, not sincerity.

Exercise: Recognize Over-the-Top Flattery

1. Think of a time someone complimented you excessively before making a request. Write down the red flags you missed.
2. List two questions you can ask yourself when faced with sudden flattery:
    - "What does this person want from me?"
    - "Does this praise feel genuine or strategic?"

Role-Playing Drill:

- Partner with a friend. One person plays the manipulator, showering compliments before making a request (e.g. "You're the best at this — can I borrow your login?").
- Practice responding with polite feedback, such as:
    - "I appreciate the compliment, but let's talk details first."

Key Takeaway

The Flattery Trap works by using excessive praise to lower your guard and manipulate trust. Enjoy genuine compliments, but stay alert when flattery feels over-the-top, especially if it's tied to a favor or request.

Chapter 25: The Greed Ploy

The Allure of Wealth

Imagine this: An email lands in your inbox claiming you've won a $1,000,000 lottery prize. The catch? You need to pay a small "processing fee" to claim it. Excited by the idea of instant wealth, you transfer the money without hesitation. Days later, you realize you've been scammed — the lottery didn't exist, and your money is gone.

This is the **Greed Ploy**, a manipulation tactic that preys on the natural human desire for wealth or rewards. Manipulators promise something extravagant and use that excitement to lure targets into giving up money, personal details, or access.

Social engineers exploit this emotional response to encourage impulsive decisions.

How It Works

1. **The Bait:** Scammers craft an irresistible reward, such as a lottery prize or a luxury giveaway.

2. **A Small "Requirement":** To claim the reward, the victim must take an action, such as paying a fee, sharing banking details, or signing a contract.
3. **The Hook:** Once the victim complies, the manipulator either disappears or continues to pressure them for more.

The Greed Ploy is especially effective because the promise of a reward overwhelms logical thinking. Victims focus on what they'll gain, not what they might lose.

Real-Life Examples

1. **Lottery Scams:** Fraudsters claim you've won a foreign lottery but require payment of a "processing fee" or taxes before you can collect your winnings.
2. **Bogus Investment Opportunities:** Manipulators promote fake schemes with impossibly high returns, luring victims into depositing money into fraudulent accounts.
3. **Social Media Giveaways:** Scammers post fake contests promising luxury prizes, requiring participants to provide personal information or pay a small fee to "enter."

Why It Works

The Greed Ploy thrives on three psychological triggers:

1. **Desire for Easy Gains:** The promise of wealth without significant effort is alluring and hard to resist.
2. **Fear of Losing Out on a Deal:** Manipulators create urgency, warning victims that the opportunity will vanish if they don't act immediately.
3. **Emotional Excitement:** The idea of winning or gaining something valuable triggers excitement, which suppresses critical thinking.

The scam works because it taps into a natural reaction: Why pass up free money or rewards?

How to Spot the Greed Ploy

1. **Too-Good-to-Be-True Offers:** Be wary of promises of wealth, high returns, or prizes that seem unrealistic or overly generous.

2. **Upfront Fees or Requirements:** Legitimate opportunities rarely require payment to claim rewards or access offers.
3. **Vague or Missing Details:** Scammers often avoid providing specifics about the reward or process, relying on excitement to obscure the lack of legitimacy.

Exercise: Test the Promise

1. Reflect on any tempting offers you've encountered—what made them appealing? Write down three red flags, such as unrealistic promises, missing verification steps, or upfront payment demands.
2. Practice responding to a fake offer by asking:
   - "Can you provide documentation proving this is legitimate?"
   - "Why do I need to pay to claim this reward?"

Role-Playing Drill:

- Partner with someone. One person plays the manipulator offering a fake prize. The other practices spotting inconsistencies and asking clarifying questions to uncover the scam.

Key Takeaway

The Greed Ploy uses the allure of riches and rewards to cloud judgment. Stay cautious when faced with offers that seem too good to be true, and remember: real opportunities don't come with strings attached.

Chapter 26: The Pride Bull's Eye

When Ego Becomes a Target

"You've been selected for our members-only program! Only the top 1% of candidates qualify." Flattered, you eagerly sign up—providing your personal details and paying a registration fee. Later, you discover the program doesn't exist, and your ego has been used against you.

This is the **Pride Bull's Eye**, a tactic where manipulators target your ego to make you feel special, chosen, or superior. By boosting your sense of importance, they lower your defenses and push you into decisions that you wouldn't make under normal circumstances.

Everyone enjoys feeling valued, especially when recognition seems earned. Social engineers exploit this universal desire for validation to manipulate trust and encourage compliance.

How It Works

1. **Flattering the Target:** Manipulators use language like "you're exceptional," "only you qualify," or "you've been specially chosen" to appeal to the victim's ego.

2. **Creating Exclusivity:** They frame the opportunity as limited, making it feel prestigious and hard to refuse.
3. **The Ask:** Once the victim is interested, the manipulator requests payment, personal information, or compliance as part of "accepting" the offer.

The Pride Bull's Eye works because people naturally want to believe they are unique, talented, or deserving of special recognition.

Real-Life Examples

1. **Fake Awards or Honors:** Scammers inform you that you've won a prestigious award but require a fee to process the recognition.
2. **Elite Job Offers:** Fraudsters offer fake leadership roles, claiming your skills are uniquely suited, and ask for your personal details or upfront fees.
3. **Invite-only Memberships:** Manipulators invite you to join groups or programs, charging steep fees for access to non-existent benefits.

Why It Works

The Pride Bull's Eye exploits three emotional drivers:

1. **Validation:** Compliments and recognition feel good, making people eager to believe and act.
2. **Fear of Missing Out:** Once the opportunity feels rare or limited, targets fear losing it by hesitating or questioning the offer.
3. **Trust in Praise:** Flattery makes victims less likely to notice red flags or inconsistencies.

The manipulator's goal is to build so much trust and excitement that the target forgets to verify the legitimacy of the offer.

How to Spot the Pride Bull's Eye

1. **Excessive Flattery:** Be cautious of compliments or recognition that feel over-the-top or unsolicited.
2. **Triggering Language:** Phrases like "only for you" or "top 1%" are often designed to trigger ego, not genuine exclusivity.

3. **Upfront Costs or Personal Information:** Legitimate honors or memberships don't require payments or sensitive details to accept.

Exercise: Test the Praise

1. Write down a situation where you were flattered into accepting an offer. Did you verify its authenticity?
2. Practice identifying red flags by asking:
    - "What makes me uniquely qualified for this?"
    - "Can I verify this opportunity through a trusted source?"

Role-Playing Drill:

- Partner with someone. One person plays the manipulator offering a flattering opportunity. The other practices responding politely:
    - "Thank you, but I'd like more details before proceeding."

Key Takeaway

The Pride Bull's Eye targets your ego to manipulate trust. Enjoy recognition, but always verify the source and remember: true exclusivity doesn't come with pressure or hidden costs.

Chapter 27: The Hope Hoax

The Trap of False Hope

Imagine you're job hunting, and an email arrives with the subject line: "We've reviewed your application, and you're an ideal candidate!" Excited, you respond. The "employer" asks for personal details or a processing fee to proceed. You comply, thinking you're about to secure your dream role—only to realize there was never a job in the first place.

This is the **Hope Hoax**, a manipulation tactic where fraudsters offer false hope, like fake jobs, scholarships, or opportunities, to exploit vulnerability. By dangling the promise of something better, manipulators gain trust and compliance.

How It Works

1. **Identify a Desire or Need:** Manipulators target individuals seeking opportunities, like employment, financial aid, or a better future.
2. **Offer the Perfect Solution:** They present an opportunity that aligns exactly with the target's goals, often through fake emails, ads, or messages.

3. **Ask for a Commitment:** Fraudsters request an action—sharing personal information, paying a fee, or signing a contract—before disappearing.

The Hope Hoax works because it preys on optimism and the desire to improve one's situation, making victims more willing to overlook red flags.

Real-Life Examples

1. **Fake Job Offers:** Scammers post listings for high-paying jobs, asking for application fees or personal details like Social Security numbers.
2. **Scholarship Scams:** Fraudsters promise financial aid or grants, requiring victims to pay upfront "processing fees."
3. **Pyramid Schemes:** Manipulators offer "can't-miss" opportunities with guaranteed high returns, stealing funds from hopeful individuals.

Why It Works

The Hope Hoax preys on three key emotions:

1. **Optimism:** Targets focus on the potential rewards, not the risks.
2. **Urgency:** Fraudsters create pressure, warning victims that the opportunity will vanish without immediate action.
3. **Validation:** Victims feel seen and valued when offered a "special opportunity," lowering their defenses.

How to Spot the Hope Hoax

1. **Too Perfect to Be True:** Be cautious of offers that match your goals exactly, especially if unsolicited.
2. **Upfront Costs or Fees:** Genuine opportunities rarely require payments or personal details upfront.
3. **Vague Details:** Fraudsters often avoid specifics, providing just enough information to seem legitimate while discouraging verification.

Exercise: Test the Opportunity

1. Write down three questions you should ask about any opportunity, like:
   - "Is this coming from a verified source?"
   - "Why is this being offered to me specifically?"
   - "Can I confirm this independently?"

Role-Playing Drill:

- Partner with someone. One person acts as the manipulator offering a fake job or scholarship. The other practices verifying the offer by asking clarifying questions and spotting inconsistencies.

Key Takeaway

The Hope Hoax uses false promises to exploit optimism. Verify every opportunity, and remember that true rewards come with transparency, not pressure.

Chapter 28: The Panic Button

The Art of Manufactured Chaos

You receive a text message: "Your bank account has been locked due to suspicious activity. Click here to secure your funds!" Panicked, you tap the link and enter your login details to resolve the issue. Moments later, your account is drained.

This is the **Panic Button**, a manipulation tactic where social engineers create fake crises to override logical thinking. By inducing fear and urgency, they force targets to act without verifying the situation.

How It Works

1. **Invent a Crisis:** Fraudsters create scenarios that trigger fear, like account breaches, unpaid fines, or safety threats.
2. **Demand Immediate Action:** They emphasize urgency to prevent victims from pausing or verifying.
3. **Offer a Solution:** Manipulators present themselves as the only way to fix the problem, pushing victims to comply.

The Panic Button works because fear activates the brain's fight-or-flight response, prioritizing quick action over critical thinking.

Real-Life Examples

1. **Fake Security Alerts:** Fraudsters send messages claiming your email or bank account has been compromised, tricking you into sharing credentials.
2. **IRS Scams:** Callers pretend to be tax authorities, threatening arrest or fines unless immediate payment is made.
3. **Emergency Phone Calls:** Scammers pose as relatives in danger, pressuring you to wire money urgently.

Why It Works

The Panic Button leverages three psychological triggers:

1. **Fear of Loss:** Victims worry about losing money, access, or safety.
2. **Time Pressure:** Urgency discourages verification or second-guessing.
3. **Trust in Solutions:** Manipulators position themselves as helpers, increasing compliance.

How to Spot the Panic Button

1. **Unverified Crises:** Be careful of replying to urgent messages about problems you didn't initiate or verify.
2. **Requests for Sensitive Details:** Legitimate organizations rarely ask for passwords, PINs, or immediate payments.
3. **Emotionally Charged Language:** Phrases like "Act Now!" or "Immediate Action Required!" are red flags.

Exercise: Pause Before Reacting

1. Write down three steps to take when you receive a crisis alert:
    - "Pause and take a deep breath."
    - "Verify the claim through official channels."
    - "Avoid clicking links or sharing details immediately."

Role-Playing Drill:

- Partner with someone. One person creates a fake crisis (e.g., "Your account has been hacked!"), while the other practices pausing, verifying, and responding calmly.

Key Takeaway

The Panic Button uses fear as a weapon. Always pause, verify the claim, and remember that real emergencies rarely require rash decisions.

Chapter 29: The Shame Shove

How Shame Becomes a Weapon

Imagine a colleague sends you an email: "I can't believe you didn't respond to my earlier request — it's so unlike you to leave things hanging!" Embarrassed, you immediately prioritize their task, even though you were unsure of its legitimacy. Later, you realize the email wasn't from your colleague — it was a scammer impersonating them, weaponizing your fear of looking unreliable.

This is the **Shame Shove**, a social engineering tactic where manipulators use embarrassment, guilt, or the fear of judgment to push you into acting. By attacking your sense of self or implying that others are watching, they make you comply to avoid further discomfort.

How It Works

1. **Targeting Self-Image:** The manipulator highlights something you "should" feel bad about, like forgetting a task or failing to respond.

2. **Implying Judgment:** They suggest that others are aware of your mistake, creating a sense of public scrutiny.
3. **Demanding Action:** They present a way to "fix" the situation, pushing you to comply quickly to restore your reputation.

The Shame Shove thrives in environments where people are eager to maintain good standing, such as workplaces, social groups, or online communities.

Real-Life Examples

1. **Impersonating Colleagues:** A scammer pretends to be your boss or co-worker, chastising you for not responding to an email and urging you to act immediately.
2. **Social Media Scams:** Fraudsters send messages like, "Your account has been flagged for inappropriate behavior—click here to avoid further embarrassment."
3. **Public Shaming Threats:** Scammers threaten to expose fabricated mistakes or secrets unless you comply with their demands.

Why It Works

The Shame Shove preys on three key emotions:

1. **Fear of Social Judgment:** People fear looking bad in front of peers, colleagues, or the public.
2. **Desire to Repair Reputation:** Shame motivates quick action to avoid further damage to self-image.
3. **Emotional Overload:** Manipulators create discomfort so intense that victims act fast to escape it.

This tactic works because the manipulator controls the narrative — whether or not the shame is justified, the target feels compelled to act.

How to Spot the Shame Shove

1. **Unverified Claims of Mistakes:** Be cautious of accusations or criticisms that seem out of character or unsubstantiated.

2. **Pressure to Comply:** Manipulators push for immediate action to prevent you from verifying the claim or calming your emotions.
3. **Focus on Reputation:** If the emphasis is on how you'll "look bad" rather than the substance of the issue, it's likely manipulation.

Exercise: Resist the Shame

1. Write down a recent situation where you felt pressured to act out of embarrassment. Reflect on whether the criticism was legitimate or manipulative.
2. Practice responding to shaming tactics with calm, clarifying questions like:
    - "Can you provide more details about the issue?"
    - "I'd like to confirm this before taking action."

Role-Playing Drill:

- Partner with someone. One person plays the manipulator, using shaming language to push compliance (e.g. "You've really let everyone down—fix this now!"). The other practices staying calm, verifying facts, and avoiding reactive decisions.

Key Takeaway

The Shame Shove uses embarrassment to override your logic and push compliance. So, remember: real accountability doesn't rely on emotional manipulation.

Chapter 30: The Empathy Bomb

The Overload of Emotion

You're scrolling through social media and come across a heart-breaking story: a family is losing their home, and they need urgent donations to keep it. Touched by the pictures and personal details, you send money immediately. Later, you find out the fundraiser was fake, and the story was a lie.

This is the **Empathy Bomb**, a tactic where manipulators overwhelm you with emotionally charged stories. By appealing to your compassion, they push you into acting impulsively — usually by donating money, sharing information, or granting access.

Empathy is a powerful human trait, but it also makes us vulnerable. When emotions take over, critical thinking takes a backseat, and manipulators exploit this to their advantage.

How It Works

1. **Crafting an Emotional Story:** The manipulator creates a compelling narrative designed to provoke sympathy or outrage.

2. **Adding Visual and Personal Touches:** They include pictures, videos, or detailed accounts to make the story feel authentic and relatable.
3. **Requesting Action:** They encourage immediate responses, like donations, information sharing, or account access, while emotions are running high.

The Empathy Bomb is especially effective in digital spaces, where visuals and stories can go viral, reaching large audiences quickly.

Real-Life Examples

1. **Fake Crowdfunding Campaigns:** Scammers create fraudulent fundraisers for fictitious victims or events, stealing money from well-meaning donors.
2. **Charity Impersonation:** Fraudsters pose as legitimate charities, using emotional appeals to solicit donations.
3. **Leveraging Emotion:** Emails with tragic stories prompt you to click links or share information to "help."

Why It Works

The Empathy Bomb exploits three psychological drivers:

1. **Compassion Fatigue:** Overexposure to emotional stories can lead to rushed actions, as victims feel pressured to help.
2. **Fear of Regret:** People will quickly make certain decisions to avoid the guilt of not helping when they could.
3. **Trust in Emotionally Charged Situations:** Emotional stories feel authentic, making victims less likely to question their legitimacy.

How to Spot the Empathy Bomb

1. **Overly Emotional Appeals:** Be cautious of stories that rely solely on tugging at your heartstrings without providing verifiable details.
2. **Urgent Requests:** Emotional manipulation often comes with immediate deadlines to prevent verification.

3. **Lack of Transparency:** Genuine organizations provide clear, traceable information about their causes and fund allocation.

Exercise: Verify Emotional Appeals

1. Reflect on a time when an emotional story influenced your actions. Did you verify the claim before responding?
2. Write down two steps to confirm legitimacy in the future, like:
   - "Research the organization or individual through trusted sources."
   - "Pause and wait 24 hours before responding."

Role-Playing Drill:

- Partner with someone. One person plays the manipulator, sharing a fake emotional story. The other practices responding with calm questions and verifying details before acting.

Key Takeaway

The Empathy Bomb overwhelms your emotions and can potentially limit logical thinking. Pause, verify the story, and remember: genuine causes welcome transparency and patience.

Chapter 31: The Anger Catalyst

How Anger Clouds Judgment

Picture this: You receive an email claiming that a company you trust has been overcharging you for years. Enraged, you click the provided link to "file a formal complaint." The page asks for your account details to "confirm your eligibility for a refund." Without hesitation, you enter the information. Minutes later, you realize you've been scammed. The company never overcharged you, and the fraudster now has your account credentials.

This is the **Anger Catalyst**, a manipulation tactic that uses outrage to overwhelm rational thinking. By provoking anger, social engineers redirect your focus to an emotional reaction, making you act impulsively rather than pausing to assess the situation critically.

How It Works

1. **Triggering Outrage:** The manipulator presents a scenario designed to provoke anger, such as injustice, unfair treatment, or betrayal.

2. **Redirecting Focus:** They make the victim so consumed with their emotional reaction that they fail to notice red flags.
3. **Encouraging Immediate Action:** The manipulator positions themselves as a solution or ally, prompting the victim to take steps like clicking a link, sharing information, or making payments.

The Anger Catalyst thrives in situations where trust has already been eroded, such as customer complaints, political discussions, or disputes.

Real-Life Examples

1. **Fake Overcharge Alerts:** Scammers claim a company has wrongfully billed you, directing you to a fraudulent site to "resolve" the issue.
2. **Outrage Campaigns:** Fraudsters post inflammatory news articles or social media posts to drive clicks, collecting data or spreading harmful files.
3. **Scam Disputes:** Fraudsters pose as mediators in disputes, gaining personal information by pretending to help victims fight back.

Why It Works

The Anger Catalyst manipulates three core human tendencies:

1. **The Need to Act:** Anger demands immediate action to address perceived wrongs, often leading to hasty decisions.
2. **Focus on the Offense:** When people are angry, their attention narrows to the source of their outrage, ignoring other details.
3. **Erosion of Critical Thinking:** Emotional intensity disrupts rational evaluation of the situation, making manipulative claims seem more credible.

Manipulators thrive on the fact that, in moments of anger, people prioritize emotional release over careful consideration.

How to Spot the Anger Catalyst

1. **Highly Emotional Messages:** Be cautious of emails, calls, or posts designed to incite outrage, especially when paired with immediate calls to action.
2. **One-Sided Information:** Anger-based tactics often focus solely on fueling your emotion without providing balanced or verifiable details.
3. **Pressure to Act Fast:** Claims like "You must act now to fix this injustice!" are often signs of manipulation.

Exercise: Pause in the Face of Anger

1. Reflect on a time when anger influenced your decisions. Write down two ways the situation could have been approached calmly.
2. Practice responding to inflammatory statements with clarifying questions like:
   - "Can you provide proof of this claim?"
   - "What steps can I take to confirm this before reacting?"

Role-Playing Drill:

- Partner with someone. One person plays the manipulator, presenting an outrageous scenario to provoke anger. The other practices staying calm and asking logical questions to regain focus.

Key Takeaway

The Anger Catalyst thrives on your emotional reaction to drive split decisions. Stay calm, verify claims, and remember: clear thinking, not anger, leads to the best solutions.

Chapter 32: The Nostalgia Smokescreen

The Power of Familiarity and Comfort

You get a call: "Remember the good old days in high school? This is Alex from your class! We're organizing a reunion and need some help reaching out." Nostalgic, you agree to share your contact list and even pay a small fee for the event. Days later, you realize there is no reunion — Alex wasn't who they claimed to be.

This is the **Nostalgia Smokescreen**, a manipulation tactic that uses fond memories and shared experiences to create trust. By evoking positive feelings from the past, manipulators create a sense of familiarity and safety, making their requests seem harmless.

How It Works

1. **Evoke Nostalgia:** The manipulator references shared experiences, trends, or items from the past that evoke positive emotions.

2. **Build a Connection:** By associating themselves with these memories, they position themselves as someone trustworthy or familiar.
3. **Make Requests:** They take advantage of the positive mood they've created.

The Nostalgia Smokescreen is particularly effective because it leverages emotions tied to the past, which are often deeply personal and comforting.

Real-Life Examples

1. **Fake Reunions:** Fraudsters pretend to be old classmates, soliciting money or information for a non-existent event.
2. **Retro Trends Scams:** Manipulators sell fake memorabilia or collect deposits for nostalgic items that are never delivered.
3. **Old-Friend Impersonation:** Scammers pose as long-lost friends, using familiarity to gain trust and ask for favors.

Why It Works

The Nostalgia Smokescreen leverages three core principles:

1. **Emotional Warmth:** Nostalgia creates positive emotions, reducing doubt.
2. **Trust Through Familiarity:** Shared memories or experiences make manipulators seem credible and safe.
3. **Focus on the Past:** Recalling memories shifts attention away from evaluating the present situation critically.

People are naturally drawn to the comfort of familiarity, which manipulators use as an entry point for their schemes.

How to Spot the Nostalgia Smokescreen

1. **Unverified Familiarity:** Be wary of messages or calls referencing shared memories that seem vague or inconsistent.
2. **Requests for Information:** Nostalgia-based tactics often lead to demands for personal details or money under the guise of reconnecting.

3. **Out-of-the-Blue Contact:** Fraudsters often initiate contact unexpectedly, counting on your surprise and positive emotions to override logical thinking.

Exercise: Question Familiarity

1. Think of a time when someone referenced your past to gain your trust. Were their claims legitimate? Write down two ways to verify such connections in the future, like asking for specific details or reaching out to a mutual contact.

Role-Playing Drill:

- Partner with someone. One person acts as a manipulator referencing a nostalgic memory. The other practices asking clarifying questions and confirming details before taking action.

Key Takeaway

The Nostalgia Smokescreen taps into fond memories to lower defenses. Always verify who you're dealing with before acting.

Chapter 33: The Curiosity Click

How Curiosity Becomes a Trap

You're browsing your inbox when a subject line catches your eye: **"Confidential Information Leaked!"** Without thinking, you click it, curious to know more. The link redirects to a suspicious page. Minutes later, your email account is compromised.

This is the **Curiosity Click**, a tactic where manipulators exploit human curiosity to encourage risky behavior. By presenting an intriguing, incomplete, or mysterious scenario, they push victims to engage before they've fully thought things through.

Curiosity drives exploration and discovery, but in the wrong hands, it can be weaponized to lead people into traps.

How It Works

1. **Create Intrigue:** Manipulators craft vague or surprising messages that spark curiosity, such as enticing subject lines, ambiguous texts, or mysterious ads.

2. **Encourage Engagement:** They provide just enough information to grab attention but withhold key details, requiring the victim to click or respond to learn more.
3. **Deliver the Payload:** Once the victim engages, they are redirected to illegally created sites or manipulated into sharing personal information.

The Curiosity Click works because humans are naturally driven to seek answers to questions or puzzles, even when they suspect potential risks.

Real-Life Examples

1. **Clickbait Emails:** Messages with subject lines like "Is This You in the Video?" trick recipients into clicking malicious links.
2. **Fake Links:** Fraudsters send texts or emails like "Your Package Has Been Delayed — Click Here for Details" to steal login credentials.
3. **Online News Scams:** Messages such as "Shocking News About [Insert Celebrity]" entice clicks, leading to fake websites that steal data or install viruses.

Why It Works

The Curiosity Click preys on three key tendencies:

1. **Need for Closure:** Humans dislike unanswered questions and are driven to resolve uncertainty.
2. **Impulse Over Caution:** Curiosity creates urgency, leading people to act before evaluating risks.
3. **Belief in Harmlessness:** Many assume "just clicking" won't cause harm, underestimating the dangers of malicious links or downloads.

Manipulators know that an intriguing question or mystery can distract targets from their better judgment.

How to Spot the Curiosity Click

1. **Vague or Sensational Messages:** Be wary of emails, ads, or messages that rely on dramatic or incomplete information.

2. **Unfamiliar Senders or Sources:** If the sender isn't someone you know or trust, avoid engaging with their message.
3. **Urgent or Emotional Appeals:** Phrases such as "Don't Miss This!" or "Urgent Action Required!" are often signs of manipulation.

Exercise: Pause Before Clicking

1. Write down three steps to evaluate a suspicious link, such as:
   - "Hover over the link to check its destination."
   - "Search for the topic independently without clicking."
   - "Verify the sender or source before engaging."

Role-Playing Drill:

- Partner with someone. One person sends a curiosity-driven message (e.g. "See This Now!"). The other practices verifying the claim before clicking or engaging.

Key Takeaway

The Curiosity Click leverages the desire for answers to prompt risky actions. Slow down, verify links and sources, and remember that not all questions need immediate answers.

Chapter 34: The Imaginary Acquaintance

The Illusion of Shared Interests

You get a message on LinkedIn: "I see you're passionate about sustainable design — I'm a big advocate too! Let's connect and collaborate." Excited by the shared interest, you respond enthusiastically and share details about your current projects. Later, you realize the person wasn't who they claimed to be. They used your interests to gain access to confidential information.

This is the **Imaginary Acquaintance**, a manipulation tactic where fraudsters pretend to share hobbies, goals, or experiences to build rapport and gain trust. By mirroring the victim's interests, they create a false sense of connection that lowers defenses.

How It Works

1. **Research the Target:** Manipulators gather information about the victim's interests, hobbies, or work through social media or public profiles.
2. **Create Common Ground:** They present themselves as sharing the same interests or goals, fostering a sense of trust and familiarity.
3. **Leverage the Connection:** Once rapport is established, they make requests for information, access, or financial help under the guise of collaboration or friendship.

The Imaginary Acquaintance is especially effective in professional or social settings, where people are eager to network or find like-minded individuals.

Real-Life Examples

1. **Professional Impersonation:** Fraudsters pretend to share professional goals to gain access to projects or systems.
2. **Social Media Scams:** Scammers pose as hobbyists or enthusiasts, joining groups or conversations to extract personal details.
3. **Phony Collaborators:** Manipulators feign interest in shared causes, like charity work, to solicit donations or favors.

Why It Works

The Imaginary Acquaintance relies on three psychological tendencies:

1. **Trust Through Similarity:** People naturally trust those who appear to share their values or interests.
2. **Desire for Connection:** Targets are more likely to engage when they believe they've found someone like-minded.
3. **Lowered Defenses:** Familiarity makes requests seem more reasonable or harmless, reducing scrutiny.

This tactic works because it feels personal. Victims believe they're interacting with someone who genuinely understands and values them.

How to Spot the Imaginary Acquaintance

1. **Unsolicited Contact:** Be cautious of people who initiate contact with overly specific claims of shared interests.
2. **Rapid Rapport Building:** Manipulators often try to create a connection quickly, skipping the natural process of getting to know someone.
3. **Requests After Bonding:** If a new "connection" starts asking for favors or access early on, it's likely manipulation.

Exercise: Verify New Connections

1. Write down three steps to confirm the authenticity of a new contact, such as:
    - "Check their social media or professional profiles for consistency."
    - "Ask clarifying questions about their background."
    - "Verify mutual connections or shared affiliations."

Role-Playing Drill:

- Partner with someone. One person plays the manipulator pretending to share an interest. The other practices identifying inconsistencies and verifying claims before engaging.

Key Takeaway

The Imaginary Acquaintance creates a false bond through shared interests. Take time to verify new connections and remember: true relationships are built on mutual trust, not fabricated familiarity.

Chapter 35: The Relationship Hijack

When Relationships Become Tools

You receive a panicked text from your sibling: "I'm stranded and need money urgently to get home. Please transfer $500 right away!" Concerned, you send the money, wanting to help. Hours later, you find out it was a scammer pretending to be them.

This is the **Relationship Hijack**, a tactic where manipulators exploit personal relationships to gain trust and compliance. By impersonating someone you care about or invoking emotional bonds, they create emotional pressure to make you act.

How It Works

1. **Impersonation:** The manipulator pretends to be a family member, partner, or friend through messages, calls, or social media.

2. **Emotional Appeal:** They frame the situation as urgent, invoking emotions such as fear, love, or guilt to gain compliance.
3. **Request for Help:** They ask for immediate assistance, such as transferring money, sharing confidential information, or granting access.

The Relationship Hijack works because it preys on trust. Relationships are deeply emotional, making people more likely to act without suspicion.

Real-Life Examples

1. **Emergency Family Scams:** Fraudsters claim to be a relative in trouble, requesting money or help to resolve fabricated emergencies.
2. **Romance Scams:** Manipulators build fake romantic relationships online, gradually gaining trust before asking for financial support or sensitive details.

Why It Works

The Relationship Hijack taps into three powerful psychological dynamics:

1. **Trust in Relationships:** People are less likely to question requests from loved ones.
2. **Fear of Letting Others Down:** Emotional appeals make targets feel obligated to help immediately.
3. **Urgency Over Verification:** The emotional weight of the situation pushes victims to act before confirming the details.

Manipulators exploit your instinct to protect and support those you care about.

How to Spot the Relationship Hijack

1. **Unexpected Requests:** Be wary of unusual messages or calls from family or friends, especially involving money or sensitive information.
2. **Urgent Tone:** Scammers often create pressure by emphasizing time-sensitive crises.
3. **Verification Resistance:** If the sender discourages you from verifying their identity, it's likely manipulation.

Exercise: Verify Relationship Requests

1. Write down two steps to confirm the authenticity of a request, like:
    - "Call the person directly using a trusted number."
    - "Ask specific questions only the real person would know."

Role-Playing Drill:

- Partner with someone. One person impersonates a loved one in trouble, while the other practices verifying the situation before acting.

Key Takeaway

The Relationship Hijack uses personal bonds to manipulate trust and urgency. Always confirm the identity of the sender and their claims before taking action.

Chapter 36: The Gratitude Debt

The Power of Reciprocity

Imagine a co-worker buys you coffee unexpectedly. Grateful, you thank them. Later, they ask, "Can you cover my shift tomorrow?" Feeling obligated to return the kindness, you agree, even though it's inconvenient.

This is the **Gratitude Debt**, a tactic where manipulators use small acts of kindness to create a sense of obligation, making their victims feel compelled to reciprocate. By initiating the cycle of reciprocity, they can extract favors, information, or compliance without arousing suspicion.

How It Works

1. **Offer a Favor:** The manipulator performs a small, unsolicited act of kindness or provides assistance.
2. **Create a Sense of Obligation:** By framing the favor as generous or thoughtful, they instill a feeling of gratitude in the target.

3. **Make a Request:** Once trust is established, they leverage the target's sense of obligation to ask for something in return — often something far greater than the original favor.

The Gratitude Debt works because humans tend to reciprocate kindness, even when the original favor was insincere or manipulative.

Real-Life Examples

1. **Workplace Manipulation:** A colleague offers to help with a project, later asking for a bigger favor, such as doing a full client pitch document that will take several days to complete.
2. **Online Scams:** Fraudsters send small, unsolicited gifts or services to users, later requesting sensitive information or monetary help.
3. **Sales Tricks:** Manipulative salespeople offer free samples or trials, pressuring targets into purchasing products they don't need.

Why It Works

The Gratitude Debt relies on three core principles of human psychology:

1. **Reciprocity Norm:** People feel a moral obligation to return kindness, even if it's disproportionate.
2. **Desire to Maintain Relationships:** Targets want to preserve goodwill and avoid appearing ungrateful.
3. **Emotional Pressure:** Gratitude clouds judgment, making targets more likely to comply without evaluating the fairness of the request.

This tactic works because people often underestimate how manipulative acts of kindness can be.

How to Spot the Gratitude Debt

1. **Unsolicited Favors:** Be cautious of unexpected acts of kindness, especially from individuals who later make demands.
2. **Disproportionate Requests:** If the repayment requested is far greater than the original favor, it's likely manipulation.

3. **Reluctance to Accept "No":** Genuine generosity doesn't come with pressure to reciprocate.

Exercise: Question Reciprocity

1. Reflect on a time when you felt obligated to repay a favor. Was the expectation fair, or did it feel manipulative? Write down ways to recognize disproportionate demands in the future.
2. Practice responding to unsolicited favors by saying:
    - "Thank you, but I prefer not to accept favors I can't easily repay."

Role-Playing Drill:

- Partner with someone. One person performs a small favor, then asks for a larger return favor. The other practices politely declining unfair demands.

Key Takeaway

The Gratitude Debt manipulates your sense of obligation through small acts of kindness. Stay aware of disproportionate requests, and remember: true generosity doesn't come with strings attached.

Chapter 37: The Exclusive Offer

How Exclusivity Opens Doors

You receive an email with the subject line: **"Congratulations! You've been selected for our VIP investment program!"** The sender claims that only a handful of elite individuals qualify for this opportunity, and you've made the cut. Flattered and intrigued, you quickly click the link and provide your personal information. Later, you discover the investment program doesn't exist, and your details have been stolen.

This is the **Exclusive Offer**, a tactic where social engineers manipulate your desire to feel special or unique by presenting fabricated opportunities. By framing these offers as exclusive and time-sensitive, they pressure victims into acting quickly, often without questioning legitimacy.

The feeling of exclusivity appeals to human psychology. People crave opportunities that make them stand out from the crowd. Manipulators exploit this need to extract compliance and gain access.

How It Works

1. **Presenting the Opportunity:** The manipulator introduces a fabricated offer, such as a VIP membership, elite program, or insider deal.
2. **Creating Scarcity:** They emphasize how rare or limited the opportunity is, making the victim feel privileged and pressured to act fast.
3. **Encouraging Immediate Action:** The victim is prompted to provide payment, sensitive details, or access to secure systems in order to "claim" the offer.

The Exclusive Offer thrives on its ability to inflate self-worth while creating urgency, reducing the likelihood of rational evaluation.

Real-Life Examples

1. **Fake Luxury Programs:** Fraudsters offer "exclusive" memberships to travel clubs, investment groups, or insider deals that require an upfront payment.
2. **Phony Job Roles:** Scammers present targets as uniquely qualified for a prestigious position, requesting application fees or personal information.

Why It Works

The Exclusive Offer exploits three key human tendencies:

1. **Desire for Recognition:** People feel validated when chosen for something rare or prestigious.
2. **Time-bound Tactics:** The emphasis on scarcity and time sensitivity encourages impulsive action.
3. **Blind Trust in Exclusivity:** Victims assume that anything labeled "exclusive" must be valuable and credible.

This tactic works because people are more likely to ignore red flags when their ego and excitement are engaged.

How to Spot the Exclusive Offer

1. **Unsolicited Recognition:** Be careful of opportunities or awards you didn't apply for or expect.
2. **Upfront Requirements:** Exclusive offers that demand immediate payment or sensitive details are often manipulative.

3. **Vague or Missing Details:** Fraudulent offers typically lack transparency about who is making the offer and why you were chosen.

Exercise: Test the Opportunity's Authenticity

1. Write down three questions to ask about any exclusive offer, such as:
    - "Why was I chosen for this opportunity?"
    - "Is there a way to verify this through official channels?"
    - "What's the catch or cost associated with accepting this?"

Role-Playing Drill:

- Partner with someone. One person presents an "exclusive offer," while the other practices asking clarifying questions and verifying details before engaging.

Key Takeaway

The Exclusive Offer plays on your desire for prestige and urgency to act. Genuine opportunities withstand scrutiny. Take the time to verify before committing.

Chapter 38: The Ticking Timer

How Time Pressure Manipulates Decisions

You're shopping online when a pop-up appears: **"Only 2 items left in stock! Sale ends in 15 minutes!"** Panicked at the thought of missing out, you rush to check out, ignoring the website's lack of security features. Moments later, you notice fraudulent charges on your card — your rush to buy led you into a scam.

This is the **Ticking Timer**, a tactic where manipulators fabricate urgency through time constraints or countdowns. By pressuring you to act immediately, they leave no room for logical evaluation, ensuring you focus only on the perceived scarcity or deadline.

Time pressure is one of the oldest tricks in the book. When urgency takes over, the brain prioritizes speed over accuracy. Manipulators capitalize on this response to trap their targets.

How It Works

1. **Fabricating Urgency:** Manipulators create artificial deadlines, warning victims that opportunities or items will disappear if they don't act quickly.
2. **Narrowing Focus:** The victim becomes consumed by the ticking clock, ignoring inconsistencies or risks.
3. **Prompting Immediate Action:** Scammers request payment, personal information, or engagement under the guise of securing the opportunity before time runs out.

The Ticking Timer relies on urgency to keep the victim emotionally engaged and mentally distracted, making it harder to notice red flags.

Real-Life Examples

1. **Flash Sales:** Fraudulent websites advertise fake discounts with countdown timers, prompting immediate purchases.
2. **Fraudulent Emails:** Scammers send messages like "Your account will be suspended in 24 hours unless you verify your details!"
3. **Crypto Scams:** Fraudsters claim that stock deals will disappear unless victims deposit money immediately.

Why It Works

The Ticking Timer leverages three psychological principles:

1. **Fear of Missing Out (FOMO):** Victims rush to secure opportunities, fearing they'll lose something valuable.
2. **Stress-Induced Focus:** Time pressure narrows attention, making victims less likely to evaluate risks or alternatives.
3. **Loss Aversion:** People are more motivated by avoiding losses than pursuing gains, making deadlines feel urgent.

This tactic works because it forces decisions in a heightened emotional state, where caution is replaced by panic.

How to Spot the Ticking Timer

1. **Unrealistic Deadlines:** Be wary of time limits that seem unusually short or aggressive, especially for major decisions.
2. **Overemphasis on Limited Availability:** Claims like "Only 1 left!" or "Act now before it's gone!" often indicate manipulation.
3. **Pressure Over Clarity:** Genuine opportunities prioritize transparency, not urgency.

Exercise: Pause Under Pressure

1. Reflect on a time when a countdown influenced your decision-making. Were the deadlines legitimate? Write down two ways you could have paused to evaluate.
2. Practice responding to artificial deadlines by saying:
   - "I'll take some time to think about this."
   - "Let me verify this claim before committing."

Role-Playing Drill:

- Partner with someone. One person plays the manipulator, using a countdown or deadline to create urgency. The other practices staying calm, asking clarifying questions, and delaying their response.

Key Takeaway

The Ticking Timer exploits urgency to suppress careful thinking. Slow down, evaluate deadlines critically, and remember: genuine opportunities allow time for consideration.

Chapter 39: The Isolation Tactic

Divide and Conquer

Imagine this: A fraudster calls pretending to be a representative from your bank. They say, "For security purposes, please don't discuss this with anyone until the issue is resolved." Feeling anxious and wanting to follow their instructions, you avoid consulting family or friends. You end up sharing sensitive details and losing money in the process.

This is the **Isolation Tactic**, where manipulators deliberately separate you from external advice or support systems, making it easier to control your decisions. By keeping you isolated, they ensure you rely solely on their guidance, which minimizes your ability to cross-check facts or recognize manipulation.

How It Works

1. **Undermine Trust in Others:** The manipulator warns the victim to avoid discussing the situation, often framing it as a matter of confidentiality or urgency.

2. **Create Dependency:** By becoming the victim's sole source of information, the manipulator positions themselves as an authority or ally.
3. **Control the Narrative:** Isolated targets are less likely to question claims, as they lack external perspectives to challenge the manipulator's story.

The Isolation Tactic works by making victims feel vulnerable and dependent on the manipulator, reducing their ability to think critically or seek help.

Real-Life Examples

1. **Romance Scams:** Manipulators in fake relationships discourage victims from sharing details with friends or family, claiming others won't understand or support them.
2. **Money Scams:** Fraudsters instruct victims to "keep this opportunity confidential" to avoid interference from third parties.
3. **Fake Emergency Calls:** Scammers warn victims not to tell anyone about the situation, claiming it will complicate or delay resolution.

Why It Works

The Isolation Tactic exploits three psychological factors:

1. **Fear of Judgment:** Victims worry that others might criticize or doubt their decisions, making them hesitant to share.
2. **Trust in Perceived Expertise:** Isolated individuals are more likely to believe the manipulator, as there's no one to challenge the claims.
3. **Reliance on Limited Information:** Without external input, victims are left with only the manipulator's narrative, making it harder to spot red flags.

Isolation allows manipulators to dominate the target's perspective, ensuring their version of events remains unchallenged.

How to Spot the Isolation Tactic

1. **Secrecy Requests:** Be cautious when someone urges you to keep information private or avoid discussing it with others.
2. **Exclusive Communication:** Manipulators often insist on being the only point of contact, discouraging second opinions.
3. **Pressure to Act Alone:** If you're being pushed to make a decision without consulting others, pause and question why.

Exercise: Break Free from Isolation

1. Write down two trusted people you could consult when faced with unusual situations. Commit to sharing concerns with them, even if someone advises against it.
2. Reflect on a time when you felt isolated in decision-making. What steps could you have taken to involve others?

Role-Playing Drill:

- Partner with someone. One person acts as the manipulator, using isolation tactics to push a decision. The other practices resisting, saying:
    - "I'd like to discuss this with someone I trust first."
    - "Why do you need me to keep this private?"

Key Takeaway

The Isolation Tactic relies on cutting off external input to control decisions. Resist secrecy and involve trusted individuals — many manipulations fall apart under shared scrutiny.

Chapter 40: The Distraction Game

Misdirection Through Overload

Picture this: You're at work juggling emails, phone calls, and a fast-approaching deadline. Suddenly, you receive an urgent message from your "IT department" requesting your login credentials to fix a critical issue. Flustered, you comply without thinking. Hours later, you discover the message was fake, and your account has been hacked.

This is the **Distraction Game**, a tactic where manipulators exploit cognitive overload to sneak past your defenses. By overwhelming your attention, they make it difficult to evaluate risks or notice inconsistencies.

When the brain is bombarded with tasks or information, it prioritizes speed over accuracy, leaving openings for manipulation.

How It Works

1. **Create Chaos:** The manipulator targets victims during high-stress or busy periods, ensuring their cognitive load is already stretched.
2. **Introduce Urgency:** They add an urgent request that demands immediate attention, further distracting the victim from evaluating the situation.
3. **Exploit the Gaps:** In the rush to respond, victims overlook red flags or procedural safeguards, giving manipulators what they need.

The Distraction Game works because people under pressure are more likely to default to reactive behaviors, such as complying without question.

Real-Life Examples

1. **Distractions During Work Hours:** Scammers send urgent emails during peak productivity times, requesting login details or payment authorizations.
2. **"IT" Scams:** Fraudsters call while victims are busy, claiming to fix a non-existent issue, distracting them from verifying the claim.
3. **Point-of-Sale Manipulation:** Retail scammers distract cashiers with questions or complaints while sneaking counterfeit bills into transactions.

Why It Works

The Distraction Game exploits three psychological vulnerabilities:

1. **Cognitive Overload:** When focus is spread thin, the brain is less effective at spotting inconsistencies or evaluating risks.
2. **Stress Response:** Pressure leads to hasty decisions, prioritizing resolution over careful thought.
3. **False Sense of Trust:** Manipulators position their request as routine or helpful, making it seem safe to comply without extra scrutiny.

This tactic is especially effective in high-pressure environments, where speed is valued over deliberation.

How to Spot the Distraction Game

1. **Poor Timing:** Think twice about requests that arrive during busy or stressful moments, especially if they demand immediate action.
2. **Out-of-Character Urgency:** Requests that deviate from normal protocols or procedures should raise suspicion.
3. **Missing Details:** Distracting tactics often rely on vague or incomplete information to exploit your rushed state.

Exercise: Slow Down Under Pressure

1. Write down three strategies to slow down and evaluate requests, such as:
    - "Take a deep breath and pause before responding."
    - "Verify the request through a trusted source."
    - "Ask clarifying questions to gather more details."

Role-Playing Drill:

- Partner with someone. One person creates a distracting scenario while making an urgent request. The other practices pausing, clarifying, and verifying before acting.

Key Takeaway

The Distraction Game thrives on overwhelming attention to obscure manipulation. Slow down, focus, and remember: most urgent requests can wait long enough for careful evaluation.

Section 3: Digital Manipulation and Online Scams

The digital age has brought unparalleled convenience — but with it, new vulnerabilities. Social engineers no longer need physical proximity to manipulate their targets; the Internet provides endless opportunities to deceive, persuade, and exploit at scale.

This section explores the most common and dangerous forms of online manipulation. By understanding how scammers operate in digital spaces, you'll learn how to recognize red flags, protect your personal information, and confidently navigate the digital landscape.

Chapter 41: The Clickbait Lure

The Psychology of Curiosity

You're scrolling through social media when a headline grabs your attention: **"Doctors Are Hiding This Simple Health Fix!"** Intrigued, you click the link, only to be bombarded by ads, dubious websites, or requests for personal details.

This is the **Clickbait Lure**, a tactic where manipulators create sensational headlines to spark curiosity and prompt clicks. Whether the goal is to collect data, or generate ad revenue, the lure succeeds because it targets one of the brain's most powerful motivators: the need to know.

How It Works

1. **Craft an Irresistible Headline:** Scammers use vague, shocking, or emotionally charged language to spark interest.
2. **Encourage Action:** The headline often ends with "Click Here" or "Find Out More," directing victims to harmful or exploitative websites.

3. **Capture Data:** Once the victim engages, the scammer extracts personal information, installs malicious software, or exploits the visitor for profit.

The Clickbait Lure works because it exploits curiosity and impatience, encouraging victims to act before evaluating the legitimacy of the source.

Real-Life Examples

1. **Fake News Links:** Fraudsters create sensational articles that redirect users to phishing or malware sites.
2. **Celebrity Hoaxes:** Headlines like "See What This Star Looks Like Now!" drive clicks to fraudulent ad-heavy websites.
3. **Health Scams:** Claims like "Doctors Warn Against This Common Food" lead to dubious pages promoting fake cures or products.

Why It Works

The Clickbait Lure exploits three psychological tendencies:

1. **Curiosity Drive:** Humans feel compelled to seek answers to incomplete or intriguing questions.
2. **Wanting to Find out News "First":** Sensational headlines create urgency, making people click before they miss the "revelation".
3. **Trust in Platforms:** People often assume that content on major platforms like Facebook or YouTube is legitimate.

How to Spot the Clickbait Lure

1. **Exaggerated Headlines:** Be wary of phrases like "You Won't Believe" or "Shocking Secrets."
2. **Low-Quality Sources:** Clickbait often comes from unfamiliar or dubious websites.
3. **Overpromises:** Headlines promising life-changing information rarely deliver legitimate content.

Exercise: Evaluate Headlines

1. Identify three headlines online that seem sensational or exaggerated. Ask yourself:
    - "Is this source credible?"
    - "What does the website gain from my click?"
2. Practice resisting the urge to click, especially on vague or shocking claims.

Role-Playing Drill:

- Partner with someone. One person creates a clickbait-style headline, while the other practices identifying red flags and avoiding engagement.

Key Takeaway

The Clickbait Lure feeds on curiosity to manipulate clicks. Pause, question the source, and remember: credible information doesn't rely on sensationalism.

Chapter 42: The Baited Email

How a Simple Email Becomes a Trap

Imagine receiving an email from what looks like an online retailer you've used before: **"Your recent order couldn't be processed. Please confirm your payment information to complete your purchase."** The email includes the retailer's logo, a detailed description of the "order," and a link to update your payment details. Frustrated and wanting to avoid delays, you click the link and enter your credit card information — only to later realize the email wasn't from the retailer at all, and your details have been stolen.

This is the **Baited Email**, a manipulation tactic where fraudsters craft deceptive emails to fool recipients. By imitating well-known companies or creating situations that demand attention, they lead victims to willingly share sensitive information or interact with malicious links.

The Baited Email succeeds because it appears professional, mimics legitimate communication styles, and creates a sense of urgency that encourages action before suspicion.

How It Works

1. **Imitating Trusted Sources:** The manipulator replicates email templates from banks, government agencies, or popular brands to create authenticity.
2. **Creating a Sense of Urgency:** Messages often warn of security risks, overdue payments, or time-sensitive opportunities, prompting recipients to act quickly.
3. **Redirecting to Fake Pages:** Links in the email direct victims to counterfeit websites that harvest sensitive information or install malicious software.

The tactic thrives because email remains a primary mode of communication, and many people aren't vigilant about verifying sender authenticity.

Real-Life Examples

1. **Account Recovery Scams:** Fraudsters claim your account has been compromised and direct you to a fake login page to "secure" it.
2. **Payment Confirmation Hoaxes:** Victims receive emails requesting payment verification for a service or subscription they never signed up for.
3. **Bogus Prize Notifications:** Emails promise rewards or cash prizes but require victims to share banking details to claim them.

Why It Works

The Baited Email leverages three psychological principles:

1. **Credibility by Design:** Familiar logos, professional language, and realistic email structures make the message appear genuine.
2. **Pressure to Act Quickly:** Threats of account suspension or missed opportunities create a sense of urgency.
3. **Convenience Bias:** Many people are used to handling account or payment issues via email – almost like everyday routine steps.

This tactic works because it seamlessly blends into the digital noise of legitimate communications, making it harder to spot.

How to Spot the Baited Email

1. **Inconsistent Email Addresses:** Check if the sender's domain matches the official organization (e.g. "@secure-payments-bank.com" vs. "@bank.com").
2. **Generic Salutations:** Phrases like "Dear Customer" instead of your actual name often indicate a scam.
3. **Unusual Requests:** Be wary of emails asking for sensitive information, especially if the request seems out of character for the organization.

Exercise: Analyze a Suspicious Email

1. Find an email you suspect might be baiting you to get personal information. Evaluate it by asking:
   - "Does the sender's address match the organization's official domain?"
   - "Does the language and tone feel professional and consistent with past emails?"
   - "Does the link's destination match what it claims to be?"
2. Practice reporting the email to your service provider or organization's security team.

Role-Playing Drill:

- Partner with someone. One person creates a baited email scenario, while the other practices identifying inconsistencies, such as strange URLs or suspicious requests.

Key Takeaway

The Baited Email preys on trust in familiar communication styles and urgency to deceive. Always verify sender details, scrutinize links, and consult official channels before taking action.

Chapter 43: The Digital Spy

Social Media: A Treasure Trove for Manipulators

Imagine you've just posted a picture from your dream vacation with the caption: **"Finally in Paris! Can't wait to spend the next two weeks exploring!"** What you don't realize is that someone with malicious intent now knows you're away from home for an extended period. While you're enjoying your trip, they could target your house or use your post to impersonate you in scams targeting your contacts.

This is the work of the **Digital Spy**, a manipulator who scours social media for information to exploit. Whether they're planning burglaries or identity theft, digital spies use the wealth of personal data available online to craft their schemes.

How It Works

1. **Gathering Data:** Digital spies monitor your posts, photos, and public profiles for information like your schedule, interests, or relationships.

2. **Analyzing Vulnerabilities:** They look for exploitable patterns, such as when you're likely to be away, your workplace habits, or details that could help bypass security questions.
3. **Targeting with Precision:** Using the information they've gathered, they create highly personalized scams, impersonations, or social engineering tactics to manipulate you or those around you.

The Digital Spy thrives because social media platforms often encourage oversharing, making it easy for manipulators to gather intelligence without detection.

Real-Life Examples

1. **Vacation Burglaries:** Criminals monitor posts about travel plans to break into homes while the owners are away.
2. **Impersonation Scams:** Fraudsters use personal details from public profiles to impersonate victims and trick their friends or family into sending money.
3. **Targeted Attacks:** Scammers tailor emails using information such as workplace details or hobbies, making their messages seem legitimate.

Why It Works

The Digital Spy exploits three key behaviors:

1. **Oversharing:** Many people share more online than they realize, including personal details such as locations, family relationships, and daily routines.
2. **Assumed Privacy:** Victims often assume their profiles are only visible to friends, overlooking privacy settings or ignoring risks of public posts.
3. **Trust in Familiarity:** Personalized scams feel more credible, making victims less likely to question their authenticity.

This tactic works because it combines publicly available data with manipulative strategies, creating a sense of legitimacy and trust.

How to Spot the Digital Spy

1. **Overly Personal Messages:** Be cautious of communications that reference specific details from your social media but come from unfamiliar sources.
2. **Unusual Activity on Your Account:** If someone accesses your profile or uses your photos, it could indicate that a digital spy is at work.
3. **Generic Profile Interactions:** Fake accounts often like, comment, or follow to gain access to your posts or earn your trust.

Exercise: Review Your Digital Footprint

1. Go through your social media profiles and list five pieces of information that could be exploited by someone with bad intentions (e.g. birthdays, vacation posts, or tagged locations).
2. Update your privacy settings to restrict who can see your posts and personal information.

Role-Playing Drill:

- Partner with someone. One person acts as a "Digital Spy," finding exploitable information from the other's public social media profile. The other practices identifying and minimizing risks.

Key Takeaway

The Digital Spy manipulates publicly available data to craft personalized schemes. Protect yourself by reviewing your privacy settings, limiting oversharing, and staying vigilant against suspicious interactions.

Chapter 44: The Untrue Profile

When Trust Is Built on a Lie

You receive a friend request from someone who claims to share your professional interests. Their profile is full of posts about industry trends and mutual connections. Thinking they could be a valuable addition to your network, you accept. Over the following weeks, they engage in friendly messages, asking questions about your work processes and suggesting collaboration opportunities. Later, you discover this person isn't real — none of your mutual connections know them either.

This is the **Untrue Profile**, a social engineering tactic where scammers create fabricated online personas to manipulate trust. These profiles are often highly convincing, using authentic-sounding bios, photos, and activity to blend seamlessly into social circles or professional networks. Once accepted, they exploit their new connection to extract sensitive information or influence decisions.

How It Works

1. **Fabricating a Digital Persona:** The manipulator crafts a profile using stock images, stolen photos, or AI-generated avatars. They pair this with a believable biography, mutual connections, and relevant posts to appear legitimate.
2. **Building Credibility:** They engage in conversations, post on relevant topics, or comment on shared interests to create a sense of authenticity.
3. **Exploiting the Relationship:** Once trust is established, they request sensitive information, propose fake opportunities, or use their connection to access more networks.

Unlike blatant scams, the Untrue Profile tactic operates slowly, relying on long-term engagement to cultivate trust before revealing manipulative intent.

Real-Life Examples

1. **Corporate Espionage:** A fake LinkedIn profile posing as a recruiter builds relationships with employees, extracting sensitive company data over time.
2. **Social Circle Infiltration:** Fraudsters create fake profiles to join private groups or gain access to personal details from a victim's friends.
3. **Networking Scams:** Manipulators use fake profiles to suggest lucrative partnerships, eventually asking for upfront payments or personal credentials.

Why It Works

The Untrue Profile exploits three psychological tendencies:

1. **Assumed Authenticity:** A well-crafted profile with a realistic photo and bio appears trustworthy.
2. **Trust in Mutuals:** Seeing shared connections or affiliations makes people more likely to accept a request without questioning its legitimacy.
3. **Desire for Opportunity:** Fake profiles often offer something valuable—such as collaboration, career advancement, or networking—enticing victims to engage.

This tactic thrives in digital spaces where interactions are often impersonal, making it easier to deceive.

How to Spot the Untrue Profile

1. **Shallow Activity:** Be cautious of profiles with limited posts, few interactions, or repetitive content.
2. **Inconsistent Details:** Fake profiles may have mismatched information, such as a bio claiming one job while posts suggest another.
3. **Excessive Friend Requests:** Scammers often connect with large numbers of people rapidly to build credibility through mutual contacts.

Exercise: Analyze a New Connection

1. Review a recent connection request on your social media. Ask yourself:
   - "Does this person have a professional history or shared background I can verify?"
   - "Are their posts and interactions consistent with a real person?"
2. Write down two ways to confirm a profile's authenticity, such as reverse image searching their profile photo or contacting mutual connections.

Role-Playing Drill:

- Partner with someone. One person acts as the creator of a fake profile, while the other practices spotting inconsistencies and verifying authenticity before connecting.

Key Takeaway

The Untrue Profile uses fabricated identities to exploit trust in online networks. Always verify connections, look for inconsistencies, and remember that not every profile is what it seems.

Chapter 45: The Malware Messenger

How a Single Click Can Open the Door

You receive an email from a colleague with the subject line: **"Important Presentation for Tomorrow – Please Review."** Inside is a friendly note: **"Let me know your thoughts on this. Thanks!"** Attached is a file labeled "presentation.pdf." Without suspecting anything, you download it. What you don't realize is that the file isn't a presentation — it's malware that silently installs on your computer, logging your keystrokes and granting access to your company's network.

This is the **Malware Messenger**, a tactic where fraudsters disguise malicious software as harmless files or links. By exploiting professional routines and trust in familiar communication, they gain access to sensitive data and systems, often without raising alarms.

How It Works

1. **Crafting the Message:** The manipulator sends emails, texts, or social media messages containing a link disguised as a legitimate URL.
2. **Enticing the Target:** The message often includes a hook, such as an unpaid invoice, a missed delivery, or an exclusive deal, to encourage clicking.
3. **Delivering the Malware:** The link downloads malicious software to the device, which can monitor activity, steal data, or lock files for ransom.

The Malware Messenger works because it combines urgency with a sense of routine, prompting victims to act without hesitation.

Real-Life Examples

1. **Fake Delivery Notifications:** Messages claim a package couldn't be delivered, directing victims to a malware-infected link.
2. **Phony Job Offers:** Fraudsters email "job applications" or "contracts" with malware embedded in the attached files.
3. **Social Media Lies:** Scammers send messages like, "Is this you in the video?" with a link to malware disguised as a social media post.

Why It Works

The Malware Messenger relies on three key vulnerabilities:

1. **Trust in Appearance:** Links and messages are often crafted to look like they come from legitimate companies or individuals.
2. **Automation Habits:** Many people reflexively click links or download attachments without inspecting them.
3. **Fear of Consequences:** Phrases like "urgent," "important," or "final notice" encourage quick action, overriding caution.

This tactic works because it exploits routine actions, such as checking messages or clicking links, to deliver harmful payloads.

How to Spot the Malware Messenger

1. **Unsolicited Messages:** Be cautious of messages from unknown sources or unexpected senders, especially those with links.
2. **Suspicious URLs:** Hover over links to verify their destination before clicking.
3. **Attachments You Didn't Request:** Avoid downloading files unless you're certain of their origin.

Exercise: Practice Safe Clicking

1. Review recent messages in your inbox or phone. Identify any that include links or attachments.
    - Ask yourself: "Am I expecting this message?"
    - Verify links by hovering over them or contacting the sender directly.
2. Write down three steps to take before clicking any link, such as inspecting the sender's address or searching for the URL online.

Role-Playing Drill:

- Partner with someone. One person creates a scenario involving a suspicious link, while the other practices identifying red flags and verifying the message before engaging.

Key Takeaway

The Malware Messenger turns routine actions into opportunities for manipulation. Always verify links and attachments before clicking, and remember: caution is your best defense against digital threats.

Chapter 46: The Passcode Pilfer

When Trust Becomes a Weakness

You're browsing online and see a message: **"Your session has expired. Please log back in to continue."** The link takes you to what looks like your email provider's login page. Without hesitation, you re-enter your credentials. A moment later, the site refreshes, and you're back on the real email homepage. What you don't realize is that you just handed your login information to a scammer.

This is the **Passcode Pilfer**, a tactic where fraudsters create deceptive scenarios to trick victims into revealing their passwords, PINs, or login credentials. By replicating trusted platforms or crafting believable situations, they gain access to sensitive accounts and systems.

How It Works

1. **Setting the Trap:** The manipulator creates a fake login page or scenario, often identical to a legitimate platform.
2. **Prompting Action:** Victims are directed to the trap via phishing emails, pop-up messages, or malicious links.

3. **Harvesting Credentials:** When victims enter their information, it's immediately recorded and used to access accounts, often without their knowledge.

The Passcode Pilfer is successful because it preys on habits — logging in feels routine, so people rarely question the process.

Real-Life Examples

1. **Fake Email Login Pages:** Scammers send emails with links to counterfeit login pages, stealing credentials as victims attempt to "verify" their accounts.
2. **Social Engineering Calls:** Manipulators call pretending to be IT support, asking for login details under the guise of fixing an issue.
3. **Public Wi-Fi Spoofs:** Fraudsters create fake Wi-Fi networks that mimic real ones, redirecting users to login pages that capture their credentials.

Why It Works

The Passcode Pilfer thrives on three factors:

1. **Visual Authenticity:** Fake login pages are often indistinguishable from real ones.
2. **Routine Behavior:** Logging in is such a common action that people rarely scrutinize the process.
3. **Fear of Inaccessibility:** Phrases like "session expired" or "account locked" prompt immediate action to regain access.

This tactic works because it turns familiar, harmless actions into moments of vulnerability.

How to Spot the Passcode Pilfer

1. **Check the URL:** Always verify that the website address matches the official domain of the platform you're using.
2. **Unexpected Prompts:** Watch out for login requests that appear suddenly or out of context.
3. **Avoid Public Logins:** Never enter credentials on public Wi-Fi networks without confirming their legitimacy.

Exercise: Verify Login Requests

1. Write down three steps to confirm the authenticity of a login page, such as:
    - Checking the website's URL for typos or inconsistencies.
    - Avoiding links from unsolicited emails or messages.
    - Navigating directly to the site through your browser instead of clicking links.

Role-Playing Drill:

- Partner with someone. One person acts as the manipulator presenting a fake login page, while the other practices identifying discrepancies and avoiding the trap.

Key Takeaway

The Passcode Pilfer exploits your trust in familiar processes to steal sensitive credentials. Always verify login pages and think critically before sharing passwords or PINs.

Chapter 47: The Catfisher

When Love Becomes a Lure

You join an online dating site and connect with someone who seems perfect. Over weeks of heartfelt conversations, they share their dreams, their struggles, and their feelings for you. They mention an emergency: **"My wallet was stolen while I was traveling. Could you send me $500 to help me get home?"** Trusting them completely, you transfer the money. Weeks later, they disappear, and you realize they were never who they claimed to be.

This is the **Catfisher**, a manipulative tactic where fraudsters pose as romantic partners to exploit emotional vulnerability. They create a false sense of intimacy, using the trust they build to ask for money, gifts, or sensitive information.

How It Works

1. **Creating a Persona:** The manipulator crafts an appealing identity, often with stolen photos and a fabricated backstory.

2. **Building a Connection:** They invest time in daily conversations, sharing fabricated details to deepen trust and emotional bonds.
3. **Exploiting Trust:** Once the relationship feels genuine, they fabricate emergencies or urgent needs, asking for financial help or personal information.

The Catfisher succeeds because they manipulate the powerful desire for connection, making their victims feel special and cared for.

Real-Life Examples

1. **Romance Scams:** Fraudsters target dating app users, developing relationships before asking for money to resolve fake crises.
2. **Military Impersonation:** Scammers pose as deployed soldiers, requesting financial assistance for fabricated expenses such as travel or medical emergencies.
3. **Cryptocurrency Investment Fraud:** After gaining trust, the manipulator suggests investing together in a "sure thing," stealing the victim's funds.

Why It Works

The Catfisher leverages three key emotional dynamics:

1. **The Need for Connection:** Victims are often lonely or seeking companionship, making them more open to emotional manipulation.
2. **Trust Through Intimacy:** Daily communication and shared "experiences" create a false sense of closeness.
3. **Urgency in Crisis:** Fake emergencies compel victims to act quickly, overriding logical thinking.

This tactic works because it exploits vulnerability and targets emotions.

How to Spot the Catfisher

1. **Too Good to Be True:** Don't trust profiles with overly perfect photos or stories that feel rehearsed or idealized.
2. **Unrealistic Situations:** Scammers often have elaborate excuses for why they can't meet in person, like being abroad or deployed.

3. **Financial Requests:** Romantic partners should never pressure you for money, especially early in a relationship.

Exercise: Verify Online Relationships

1. Write down three ways to confirm someone's identity, such as:
   - Conducting a reverse image search of their profile photo.
   - Asking for a video chat to ensure they match their profile.
   - Involving a trusted friend to help evaluate their claims.

Role-Playing Drill:

- Partner with someone. One person pretends to be a Catfisher, creating a scenario where they request money. The other practices identifying red flags and refusing the request.

Key Takeaway

The Catfisher exploits emotional vulnerability to build trust and manipulate. Protect yourself by verifying online connections and remembering that true relationships don't involve financial pressure.

Chapter 48: The Deepfake Puppeteer

The Deceptive Face of AI

You receive a personalized voicemail from a well-known charity: **"This is Emma Jones, our outreach director. We're raising urgent funds for disaster relief. As one of our loyal donors, can we count on you for a $1,000 contribution today?"** The voice sounds warm and familiar, and they reference your past donation details. You quickly transfer the money. Days later, you learn the charity never contacted you. The voicemail was a deepfake designed to impersonate the outreach director and exploit your goodwill.

This is the **Deepfake Puppeteer**, where scammers use AI-generated voices, videos, or photos to impersonate trusted individuals or organizations. By mimicking real people with uncanny accuracy, they manipulate their targets into taking actions they wouldn't otherwise consider.

How It Works

1. **Collecting Data:** The manipulator gathers publicly available videos, photos, or recordings of the target.
2. **Creating the Deepfake:** Using AI tools, they generate convincing fake content that replicates the target's appearance or voice.
3. **Deploying the Manipulation:** The deepfake is used to make demands, spread misinformation, or impersonate someone in a position of trust.

The Deepfake Puppeteer is particularly dangerous because of the growing accessibility of AI tools, making it easier than ever to create convincing fake content.

Real-Life Examples

1. **Impersonation for Fraud:** Scammers use deepfake videos of executives to instruct employees to transfer funds or reveal sensitive information.
2. **Extortion Scams:** Fraudsters create fake compromising videos of victims and threaten to release them unless they're paid.
3. **Disinformation Campaigns:** Manipulators use deepfakes to spread false statements attributed to public figures, causing confusion or panic.

Why It Works

The Deepfake Puppeteer preys on three vulnerabilities:

1. **Trust in Visuals:** People are conditioned to believe what they see, making realistic deepfakes highly convincing.
2. **Reliance on Authority:** Victims often comply with requests from individuals they recognize or respect.
3. **Lack of Awareness:** Many people are unfamiliar with the capabilities of deepfake technology, making them more susceptible.

This tactic works because it combines advanced technology with psychological manipulation, creating a powerful illusion of authenticity.

How to Spot the Deepfake Puppeteer

1. **Unusual Requests:** Watch out for unexpected demands, even from familiar faces or voices.
2. **Minor Inconsistencies:** Deepfakes may show subtle visual glitches, such as unnatural lighting or awkward facial movements.
3. **Verify Through Other Channels:** Always confirm requests through a separate method, such as a phone call or email.

Exercise: Test for Deepfakes

1. Write down two ways to verify a video or audio message, such as:
    - Asking follow-up questions only the real person would know.
    - Checking for irregularities like unnatural speech patterns or mismatched visuals.
2. Practice verifying requests by using alternative communication channels before acting.

Role-Playing Drill:

- Partner with someone. One person creates a deepfake scenario (e.g. posing as a boss or colleague), while the other practices verifying the authenticity of the message before responding.

Key Takeaway

The Deepfake Puppeteer uses advanced AI to impersonate trusted individuals and manipulate victims. Always verify requests, and remember: even convincing visuals can be deceptive.

Chapter 49: The Privacy Blackmail Trap

How Fear and Privacy Collide

One morning, you open your inbox to a shocking message: **"We've accessed your webcam and recorded compromising footage of you. Unless you send $1,500 in Bitcoin within 48 hours, the video will be sent to your contacts."** Panicked, you check the email's details. It even includes a password you once used, making it feel credible. You debate paying to avoid the embarrassment, but the footage never existed. The email was a bluff designed to manipulate your fear.

This is the **Privacy Blackmail Trap**, a tactic where scammers use either fabricated claims or real stolen information to extort money. The threat of exposure, even if baseless, is often enough to drive victims to comply.

How It Works

1. **Stolen or Fake Data:** Manipulators use hacked passwords, email addresses, or vague personal details to appear credible.
2. **Fabricated Scenarios:** They create alarming but false claims, such as hacked webcams or private file access, to induce panic.
3. **Demanding Ransom:** Victims are instructed to pay a sum — usually in untraceable cryptocurrency — to prevent the fabricated "leak."

The Privacy Blackmail Trap works because it targets deeply personal fears, exploiting the human need to protect one's reputation and relationships.

Real-Life Examples

1. **Webcam Scams:** Fraudsters claim to have recorded compromising footage via the victim's device and demand payment to suppress it.
2. **Hacked Email Threats:** Scammers send emails containing passwords obtained from data breaches to convince victims they've been hacked.
3. **Fake Evidence Manipulation:** Manipulators create fake "evidence" such as doctored images or videos to pressure victims into compliance.

Why It Works

The Privacy Blackmail Trap manipulates three powerful fears:

1. **Fear of Exposure:** Victims often panic at the thought of their private lives being made public.
2. **Belief in Specific Details:** The inclusion of stolen passwords or personal data makes the threat feel real.
3. **Urgency Under Pressure:** Threats with deadlines ("48 hours to respond") drive rushed decisions.

This tactic is successful because victims often act out of fear rather than taking time to verify the scam.

How to Spot the Privacy Blackmail Trap

1. **Simplistic Language:** Scammers often use vague claims that don't specify any actual private details.
2. **Data From Old Breaches:** Check if the passwords they mention are outdated or from known data leaks.
3. **Unreasonable Requests:** Demands for cryptocurrency payments are a major red flag.

Exercise: Protect Your Privacy

1. Search online to see if your email address or passwords appear in any recent data breaches. Change compromised passwords immediately.
2. Write down three actions to safeguard your online privacy, such as:
   - Using a password manager to create unique passwords.
   - Enabling two-factor authentication for all accounts.
   - Covering your webcam when not in use.

Role-Playing Drill:

- Partner with someone. One person pretends to be a scammer using vague threats of exposure, while the other practices staying calm, verifying the claim, and refusing to engage.

Key Takeaway

The Privacy Blackmail Trap relies on fear and urgency to manipulate victims. Verify all claims, secure your accounts, and remember: real hackers don't send warnings.

Chapter 50: The Ransomware Ruse

How Ransomware Takes Control

You open an email from what appears to be your IT department: **"Please update your system with this security patch immediately."** Trusting the message, you download the attachment. Moments later, your computer locks up, and a terrifying message appears: **"Your files have been encrypted. Pay $5,000 in Bitcoin to recover them."** Panicked, you realize all your data — photos, work documents, and personal files — are inaccessible.

This is the **Ransomware Ruse**, where scammers infect a victim's device with malicious software that encrypts files, making them inaccessible. They demand payment in exchange for a decryption key, preying on the victim's desperation to regain control of their data.

How It Works

1. **Delivery of Harmful Files:** Ransomware is typically installed through email attachments, fake software updates, or malicious websites.
2. **Encrypting Files:** Once activated, critical files are locked, often including backups, rendering them unusable.
3. **Demanding Payment:** Victims receive instructions to pay a ransom — usually in cryptocurrency — in exchange for the decryption key.

The Ransomware Ruse succeeds because it targets both individual users and organizations, where the loss of critical data can have devastating consequences.

Real-Life Examples

1. **Hoax Emails:** Fraudsters disguise ransomware as email attachments, such as invoices or resumes, tricking victims into downloading it.
2. **Fake Software Updates:** Scammers create pop-ups urging users to install "updates" that deliver ransomware instead.
3. **Targeted Attacks on Businesses:** Cybercriminals target companies, locking entire networks and demanding large sums to restore operations.

Why It Works

The Ransomware Ruse exploits three core vulnerabilities:

1. **Dependence on Digital Data:** Victims fear losing irreplaceable files, such as business records or personal photos.
2. **Lack of Preparedness:** Many users and companies lack secure backups, making them more likely to comply with ransom demands.
3. **Panic-Induced Decisions:** The pressure of a ticking deadline drives victims to pay rather than explore alternatives.

This tactic works because it combines fear, urgency, and technical barriers, making victims feel helpless.

How to Spot the Ransomware Ruse

1. **Unsolicited Attachments:** Be wary of unexpected emails with attachments or links, especially from unknown senders.
2. **Pop-Up Urgency:** Avoid clicking on pop-ups claiming your system needs immediate updates.
3. **Encrypted Files Without Warning:** If your files suddenly become inaccessible, ransomware may be the cause.

Exercise: Build a Ransomware Defense

1. Write down three steps to protect against ransomware attacks, such as:
    - Regularly backing up important files to an external device.
    - Keeping all software and antivirus programs up to date.
    - Avoiding suspicious links and attachments.

Role-Playing Drill:

- Partner with someone. One person plays the role of a scammer delivering ransomware through a fake email, while the other practices identifying red flags and safely handling the situation.

Key Takeaway

The Ransomware Ruse manipulates your dependency on digital files to demand payment. Protect yourself by maintaining secure backups, avoiding suspicious downloads, and staying vigilant against fake updates.

Chapter 51: The Subscription Steal

How Subscriptions Become Scams

You receive an email with the subject line: **"Action Required: Your Subscription Is About to Expire."** The sender appears to be a trusted streaming service such Spotify or Netflix, and the email includes a link to "renew" your subscription. Concerned about losing access, you click the link, enter your credit card information, and confirm payment. Later, you notice unauthorized charges on your card. The email wasn't from the service, and your details are now in the hands of a scammer.

This is the **Subscription Steal**, a tactic where fraudsters create fake renewal notifications to trick victims into sharing payment information. By preying on the fear of losing access to services, they exploit quick reactions to extract financial details.

How It Works

1. **Creating Fake Notifications:** The manipulator sends realistic-looking emails, texts, or app notifications mimicking trusted services.
2. **Pressuring Immediate Action:** Victims are urged to "renew" to avoid service disruption, often with phrases such as "urgent" or "final notice."
3. **Harvesting Financial Data:** Links lead to counterfeit payment pages where victims unknowingly submit their credit card information.

The Subscription Steal thrives on routine habits — most people don't think twice about renewing a service they use regularly.

Real-Life Examples

1. **Streaming Service Scams:** Fraudsters impersonate platforms such as Prime or Disney+, sending fake renewal emails to collect payment details.
2. **Software Licensing Fraud:** Emails claiming software licenses are expiring lead victims to phishing sites.
3. **App Store Renewal Hoaxes:** Scammers mimic app store notifications to trick users into updating billing information.

Why It Works

The Subscription Steal manipulates three key behaviors:

1. **Trust in Familiar Services:** Victims are less suspicious when messages appear to come from brands they use daily.
2. **Routine Compliance:** People are accustomed to renewing subscriptions, making fake requests feel normal.
3. **Fear of Losing Access:** The threat of losing a valued service drives victims to act quickly without verifying authenticity.

This tactic works because it blends seamlessly into the constant flow of legitimate subscription updates.

How to Spot the Subscription Steal

1. **Check the Sender's Details:** Scammers often use email addresses or domains that are close but not identical to official ones.
2. **Verify Links:** Hover over links to see where they lead — legitimate services will always use their official domain.
3. **Inspect the Message:** Look for typos, simplified greetings, or inconsistent branding, which are common in fake notifications.

Exercise: Review Subscription Emails

1. Find a recent subscription-related email in your inbox. Ask yourself:
    - "Is the sender's address authentic?"
    - "Does the email request action through a third-party link?"
2. Practice logging into the service directly instead of clicking links in the email to confirm its legitimacy.

Role-Playing Drill:

- Partner with someone. One person acts as the manipulator creating a fake renewal notice, while the other practices identifying inconsistencies and verifying through official channels.

Key Takeaway

The Subscription Steal exploits trust in everyday services to collect financial information. Always verify renewal notices by logging into your account directly and avoid acting on unsolicited messages.

Chapter 52: The Survey Snare

When a Survey Is More Than It Seems

You see a social media post: **"Complete our quick survey and win a $100 gift card!"** The link leads to a professional-looking questionnaire asking for your name, email, date of birth, and even partial credit card details to verify your "eligibility." Excited about the reward, you provide the information. Weeks later, you realize your identity has been stolen and used to open unauthorized accounts.

This is the **Survey Snare**, a tactic where scammers create fake polls or surveys to trick victims into willingly sharing personal and financial information. By disguising their schemes as harmless questionnaires, they make the scam appear legitimate and enticing.

How It Works

1. **Crafting the Survey:** The manipulator designs a believable poll or questionnaire, often hosted on fake but professional-looking websites.

2. **Incentivizing Participation:** Victims are promised rewards like gift cards, discounts, or prizes for completing the survey.
3. **Harvesting Data:** The survey collects personal information under the guise of eligibility or verification requirements.

The Survey Snare works because people are accustomed to filling out surveys for promotions or feedback, lowering their guard.

Real-Life Examples

1. **Fake Gift Card Surveys:** Fraudsters offer gift cards for popular retailers in exchange for completing surveys that collect sensitive data.
2. **Social Media Poll Scams:** Manipulators share links to surveys claiming to support charities, using them to harvest personal information.
3. **Event Feedback Fraud:** Fake surveys about recent events or purchases trick victims into sharing unnecessary details.

Why It Works

The Survey Snare exploits three common tendencies:

1. **Appeal of Rewards:** The promise of free items or discounts encourages victims to participate without questioning the source.
2. **Normalization of Surveys:** Victims often associate surveys with legitimate feedback or promotions, making them more susceptible to being tricked.
3. **Assumption of Harmlessness:** Filling out forms feels routine, so people rarely consider the risks of sharing data.

This tactic works because it disguises exploitation as an everyday activity.

How to Spot the Survey Snare

1. **Too-Good-To-Be-True Rewards:** Be cautious of surveys promising unusually high-value rewards for minimal effort.

2. **Unfamiliar Links:** Verify the website hosting the survey to ensure it is associated with a legitimate organization.
3. **Excessive Data Requests:** Legitimate surveys rarely ask for sensitive information like credit card numbers or social security details.

Exercise: Evaluate a Survey

1. Find a survey online and ask yourself:
   - "Is this survey hosted on a trusted website?"
   - "Am I being asked for information beyond what's necessary?"
2. Practice researching the organization offering the survey to confirm its legitimacy.

Role-Playing Drill:

- Partner with someone. One person creates a fake survey scenario, while the other practices identifying red flags and verifying its authenticity before participating.

Key Takeaway

The Survey Snare uses fake polls to collect sensitive information. Always verify the source, question the reward's legitimacy, and avoid sharing unnecessary details.

Chapter 53: The Bogus Giveaway

When "Free" Comes at a Cost

You're scrolling through social media when you see a post: **"We're giving away 10 new laptops to celebrate our anniversary! Enter by clicking here!"** The link takes you to a sleek website with a form where you are required to fill in your personal details, including your address and payment information for a "small shipping fee." Days later, you notice unauthorized charges on your credit card — and realize the giveaway was a scam.

This is the **Bogus Giveaway**, a tactic where scammers lure victims with fake prize offers to steal their personal information or money. By combining excitement with a sense of urgency, they trick victims into taking quick, unverified actions.

How It Works

1. **Designing the Trap:** Manipulators create professional-looking ads or websites promising free prizes such as electronics, gift cards, or cash.
2. **Requiring Details to "Claim" the Prize:** Victims are asked to fill out forms with personal or financial information, often under the guise of verifying eligibility.
3. **Exploiting the Data:** The information is either sold, used for identity theft, or used to charge victims fraudulent fees.

The Bogus Giveaway thrives because it preys on people's excitement over winning something valuable for "free."

Real-Life Examples

1. **Fake Tech Giveaways:** Scammers promise free gadgets such as smartphones or tablets, requiring credit card details for shipping costs.
2. **Social Media Contests:** Fraudsters use fake brand pages to promote giveaways, harvesting data from participants.
3. **Email Sweepstakes Hoaxes:** Emails claim you've won a cash prize or luxury vacation, asking for bank details to "transfer the funds."

Why It Works

The Bogus Giveaway exploits three key tendencies:

1. **Excitement Over Rewards:** The allure of winning a high-value item creates emotional engagement, making people throw caution to the wind.
2. **Trust in Familiar Brands:** Fake giveaways often mimic reputable companies, making them seem legitimate.
3. **Time Pressure:** Countdown timers or limited-entry claims pressure victims into acting without verifying the offer.

This tactic works because it manipulates emotions, encouraging impulsive decisions that bypass logic.

How to Spot the Bogus Giveaway

1. **Verify the Source:** Check if the giveaway is hosted on the official website or social media page of the company.
2. **Excessive Information Requests:** Be cautious if the giveaway asks for sensitive details like your address, credit card, or social security number.
3. **Unrealistic Rewards:** High-value prizes for minimal effort (e.g. "Just click to win a car!") are often too good to be true.

Exercise: Evaluate a Giveaway Offer

1. Find an online giveaway and assess its legitimacy by asking:
   - "Is this hosted by the company's official website or page?"
   - "Am I being asked for unnecessary information or payment?"
2. Practice looking for reviews or warnings about the giveaway online to confirm whether it's legitimate.

Role-Playing Drill:

- Partner with someone. One person presents a fake giveaway scenario, while the other practices identifying red flags and verifying the offer before engaging.

Key Takeaway

The Bogus Giveaway manipulates excitement and urgency to extract personal details or money. Verify all offers, and remember: genuine giveaways never ask for sensitive information or payment to claim a prize.

Chapter 54: The Support Scam

When Help Becomes a Hoax

You're working on your computer when your phone rings. The caller introduces themselves as a representative from your Internet provider: **"We've detected unusual activity on your network, which may have compromised your security. We need to fix it immediately."** They guide you through installing software, claiming it will resolve the issue. However, this program isn't protective — it grants them full access to your computer. Moments later, they demand a fee for "fixing" the problem, or worse, they start transferring your personal data.

This is the **Support Scam**, a tactic where fraudsters impersonate technical support to exploit trust. By using convincing jargon and creating urgency, they trick victims into granting access to devices or paying for non-existent repairs.

How It Works

1. **Creating the Alarm:** Scammers use pop-ups, fake error messages, or unsolicited calls to convince victims their devices are at risk.

2. **Establishing Credibility:** Posing as legitimate support staff, they use technical jargon to gain the victim's trust.
3. **Gaining Access or Payment:** Victims are persuaded to install remote access software or pay for unnecessary services.

The Support Scam succeeds because most people lack the technical knowledge to identify whether the issue is real.

Real-Life Examples

1. **Fake Microsoft Support:** Scammers cold-call victims, claiming to be from Microsoft and offering to "fix" non-existent issues.
2. **Pop-Up Warning Scams:** Fraudulent ads display warnings about supposed infections, directing victims to fake support hotlines.
3. **Payment for Useless Services:** Victims are charged for "repairs" that don't solve any actual problems.

Why It Works

The Support Scam relies on three main strategies:

1. **Creating Fear:** Alarming messages or calls make victims panic, prompting them to act quickly.
2. **Appearing Professional:** The use of technical terms and convincing scripts builds credibility.
3. **Exploiting Confusion:** Most people don't understand how to verify technical issues, making them vulnerable to manipulation.

This tactic works because it turns unfamiliarity with technology into a gateway for exploitation.

How to Spot the Support Scam

1. **Unsolicited Communication:** Be suspicious of unexpected pop-ups or calls claiming your device has issues.
2. **Pressure to Act Quickly:** Scammers often emphasize urgency to prevent victims from seeking a second opinion.

3. **Requests for Remote Access:** Legitimate support rarely requires you to install software or grant remote control without prior contact.

Exercise: Respond to a Fake Support Call

1. Write down two responses to unsolicited tech support claims, such as:
   - "I'll contact my device's official support team directly."
   - "Please provide documentation of the issue you're referring to."
2. Practice refusing remote access or payments when pressured by someone claiming to be from technical support.

Role-Playing Drill:

- Partner with someone. One person plays a fake support agent, while the other practices staying calm, verifying the claims, and refusing access or payment.

Key Takeaway

The Support Scam exploits fear and confusion about technology to gain access or money. Verify all technical issues through official channels and never allow unsolicited remote access.

Chapter 55: The Trojan Ad

When Ads Turn Dangerous

You're browsing your favorite news site when a colorful ad catches your eye: **"Win a Trip to Hawaii! Click Here to Claim!"** The ad looks legitimate, and the site hosting it is trusted, so you click. Instantly, your computer slows down, and pop-ups start appearing. Unbeknownst to you, clicking the ad installed malware designed to track your activities and extract sensitive data such as passwords and payment details.

This is the **Trojan Ad**, a tactic where scammers embed malicious code into online advertisements. By disguising malware within enticing banners or pop-ups, they exploit trust in websites and users' curiosity to infect devices.

How It Works

1. **Planting the Ad:** Fraudsters create ads with embedded malicious code, often using trusted ad networks to distribute them.

2. **Enticing the Victim:** Ads are designed to attract attention with appealing offers, such as prizes, discounts, or urgent warnings.
3. **Triggering Malware:** Clicking the ad activates hidden code, which downloads malware, such as spyware or ransomware, onto the victim's device.

The Trojan Ad succeeds because users often associate ads with promotions rather than threats, making them less cautious.

Real-Life Examples

1. **Fake Prize Ads:** Ads offering vacations, cash, or electronics lead to sites that install spyware or steal credentials.
2. **Malicious Pop-Ups:** Fraudsters design pop-ups claiming the victim's device has a virus, tricking them into clicking for "solutions."
3. **Infected Ad Networks:** Even legitimate websites sometimes unknowingly host Trojan Ads through compromised ad services.

Why It Works

The Trojan Ad relies on three key vulnerabilities:

1. **Trust in Websites:** Users assume ads on trusted sites are vetted, reducing their suspicion of malicious content.
2. **Attraction to Deals:** Promises of free rewards or exclusive offers prompt quick clicks.
3. **Technical Invisibility:** Embedded malware operates silently, often going undetected until it's too late.

This tactic works because it disguises danger as an opportunity, blending seamlessly into the digital landscape.

How to Spot the Trojan Ad

1. **Too-Good-To-Be-True Offers:** Be cautious of ads promising significant rewards for minimal effort.
2. **Unexpected Pop-Ups:** Ads claiming urgent action is required, such as fixing a virus, are often malicious.

3. **Unfamiliar Sources:** Hover over ad links to check the URL before clicking — legitimate ads lead to recognizable domains.

Exercise: Practice Safe Browsing

1. Visit a trusted site with ads. Hover over several ads without clicking, and ask yourself:
    - "Does this offer seem realistic?"
    - "Is the URL trustworthy?"
2. Write down two strategies to avoid Trojan Ads, such as using an ad blocker or avoiding ads entirely.

Role-Playing Drill:

- Partner with someone. One person creates a fake scenario involving a tempting ad, while the other practices identifying and avoiding it.

Key Takeaway

The Trojan Ad hides malicious intent within seemingly harmless promotions. Avoid clicking ads from unverified sources, and use security measures such as ad blockers and antivirus software to stay protected.

Chapter 56: The Public Wi-Fi Trap

How Public Convenience Becomes a Threat

You're at the airport and connect to the free public Wi-Fi to check your bank account. Everything seems normal until days later, when you notice unauthorized transactions. Unbeknownst to you, a hacker using the same network intercepted your login credentials using a technique called a "man-in-the-middle" attack.

This is the **Public Wi-Fi Trap**, where scammers exploit insecure networks to steal data. By eavesdropping on unencrypted traffic, they can intercept passwords, credit card numbers, and other sensitive information.

How It Works

1. **Setting the Trap:** Fraudsters connect to public Wi-Fi networks or create fake hotspots with similar names to legitimate ones.
2. **Monitoring Activity:** They use software to intercept unencrypted data transmitted over the network, such as login credentials or personal information.

3. **Exploiting the Data:** Stolen information is used for identity theft, account breaches, or financial fraud.

The Public Wi-Fi Trap succeeds because most users assume public networks are secure and don't take precautions.

Real-Life Examples

1. **Fake Hotspots:** Hackers create Wi-Fi networks with names like "Airport Free Wi-Fi" to trick users into connecting.
2. **Man-in-the-Middle Attacks:** Fraudsters intercept data on legitimate public networks, stealing passwords and other details.
3. **Session Hijacking:** Scammers take control of active sessions, such as email or social media accounts, by stealing cookies.

Why It Works

The Public Wi-Fi Trap exploits three common behaviors:

1. **Assumption of Security:** Many people assume public networks are safe because they're widely used.
2. **Lack of Encryption:** Unencrypted connections make it easy for hackers to intercept data.
3. **Convenience Over Caution:** Users prioritize quick access over secure browsing when connecting to public Wi-Fi.

This tactic works because it leverages routine actions, such as checking emails or making transactions, to extract sensitive information.

How to Spot the Public Wi-Fi Trap

1. **Unfamiliar Networks:** Be wary of networks with generic names or those that don't require a password.
2. **Unencrypted Connections:** Avoid websites without HTTPS (the padlock icon) when using public Wi-Fi.
3. **Suspicious Activity:** If a network suddenly disconnects and reconnects, it could be a sign of tampering.

Exercise: Practice Safe Wi-Fi Usage

1. Write down three strategies for secure browsing on public Wi-Fi, such as:
   - Using a virtual private network (VPN) to encrypt your data.
   - Avoiding financial transactions on public networks.
   - Disconnecting from public Wi-Fi when not in use.
2. Check your device settings to ensure it doesn't automatically connect to unfamiliar networks.

Role-Playing Drill:

- Partner with someone. One person plays a hacker setting up a fake hotspot, while the other practices identifying and avoiding insecure networks.

Key Takeaway

The Public Wi-Fi Trap manipulates the convenience of free networks to steal sensitive data. Always use encryption, verify networks, and limit sensitive activity when connected to public Wi-Fi.

Chapter 57: The QR Code Con

When Convenience Becomes a Trap

You're at a restaurant, and the menu includes a QR code for easy access to their online ordering system. Without thinking, you scan it and land on what looks like their website. It asks you to log in with your email and password, so you do. Later, you notice unauthorized activity in your accounts. The QR code wasn't placed by the restaurant — it was a fake notice applied by a scammer to harvest your credentials.

This is the **QR Code Con**, a tactic where fraudsters manipulate the trust and convenience of QR codes to misdirect users to malicious websites. By altering legitimate-looking codes or planting fake ones, they exploit your willingness to engage without verifying.

How It Works

1. **Planting the Code:** Scammers place fake QR code stickers on posters, menus, or advertisements. These codes redirect users to malicious sites or initiate unauthorized downloads.

2. **Exploiting Trust:** Victims assume the QR code is legitimate, especially if it's placed in trusted environments like restaurants or public transport.
3. **Stealing Data or Delivering Dangerous Software:** Once the victim scans the code, they're tricked into sharing credentials, financial details, or unknowingly downloading malware.

The QR Code Con thrives because QR codes are quick and easy to use, and most people rarely verify their source.

Real-Life Examples

1. **Fake Menu Codes:** Fraudsters replace QR codes on restaurant menus with their own, redirecting customers to phishing sites.
2. **Parking Payment Scams:** Fake QR codes placed on parking meters lead users to fraudulent payment portals.
3. **Event Ticketing Hoaxes:** QR codes on counterfeit tickets direct victims to infected sites.

Why It Works

The QR Code Con exploits three key behaviors:

1. **Assumption of Authenticity:** QR codes are seen as harmless, especially when used in professional settings.
2. **Speed Over Caution:** Scanning a code feels routine, making users less likely to pause and verify.
3. **Trust in Appearance:** Codes are easy to replicate, and fake ones often look identical to legitimate codes.

This tactic works because it leverages convenience and disguises itself within trusted environments.

How to Spot the QR Code Con

1. **Inspect the Code:** Check for signs of tampering, such as stickers placed over original codes.
2. **Be Wary of Shortened Links:** Scammers often use shortened URLs to hide the true destination of their fake QR codes.

3. **Verify the Source:** Confirm with the business or organization that the QR code is legitimate before scanning.

Exercise: Evaluate QR Code Safety

1. Locate a QR code you've recently scanned and ask:
   - "Was it placed in a secure location?"
   - "Did I verify the organization behind it?"
2. Practice using a QR scanner app that shows the URL before opening it, allowing you to verify the destination.

Role-Playing Drill:

- Partner with someone. One person sets up a fake QR code scenario, while the other practices identifying red flags and verifying legitimacy before scanning.

Key Takeaway

The QR Code Con turns convenience into a weapon for scams. Always inspect QR codes for authenticity, verify their sources, and be cautious of shortened or unfamiliar URLs.

Chapter 58: The Crypto Trap

How Promises of Wealth Become a Trap

A friend excitedly shares a new cryptocurrency platform, claiming, **"I made $5,000 in just two days — this is your chance to get in early!"** They show you a professional-looking website filled with testimonials and graphs of rising profits. You invest $1,000, and at first, your account shows rapid growth. But when you try to withdraw your earnings, you're told you need to deposit more money to "unlock" your funds. Days later, the website disappears, along with your investment.

This is the **Crypto Trap**, a scheme where scammers exploit the buzz around cryptocurrency to deceive victims. By promising high returns, leveraging fear of missing out, and creating fake platforms, they lure individuals into fraudulent investments.

How It Works

1. **Setting the Hook:** Scammers create professional-looking websites or social media accounts to advertise "once-in-a-lifetime" cryptocurrency opportunities.

2. **Building Trust:** They use fake testimonials, doctored screenshots of profits, and even paid influencers to make the scheme seem credible.
3. **Stealing Investments:** Victims deposit funds into the fake platform, which is then siphoned off by the scammers. Attempts to withdraw funds are blocked or require additional payments.

The Crypto Trap works because cryptocurrency is complex and poorly understood by many, making it easier to deceive victims with jargon and promises.

Real-Life Examples

1. **Ponzi Crypto Schemes:** Scammers use funds from new investors to pay "returns" to earlier ones, creating the illusion of success.
2. **Fake ICOs (Initial Coin Offerings):** Fraudsters create fake cryptocurrencies, convincing victims to buy tokens that are worthless.
3. **Phishing Wallet Scams:** Victims are tricked into entering their wallet credentials on fake platforms, allowing scammers to steal their funds.

Why It Works

The Crypto Trap leverages three main factors:

1. **Promise of High Returns:** Victims are drawn to the idea of making significant profits in a short time.
2. **Trust in Trends:** The popularity and complexity of cryptocurrency make scams appear legitimate.
3. **Fear of Missing Out:** Exclusive "early access" opportunities push victims to act without researching.

This tactic works because it combines confusion about cryptocurrency with psychological pressure to act quickly.

How to Spot the Crypto Trap

1. **Verify Platforms:** Check if the platform is registered or reviewed by credible financial authorities.
2. **Avoid Unrealistic Promises:** Be cautious of platforms guaranteeing massive profits or "risk-free" investments.

3. **Watch for Withdrawal Restrictions:** Legitimate platforms don't block access to your funds or require extra payments to withdraw.

Exercise: Research a Crypto Investment

1. Find a cryptocurrency platform and research its credibility by asking:
    - "Is this platform regulated by a recognized authority?"
    - "Are the testimonials and reviews consistent and verifiable?"
2. Practice searching for red flags like fake reviews or unreasonably high returns.

Role-Playing Drill:

- Partner with someone. One person pitches a fake crypto investment, while the other practices asking critical questions and verifying its legitimacy.

Key Takeaway

The Crypto Trap exploits the buzz and confusion around cryptocurrency to deceive victims. Avoid platforms with unrealistic promises, verify credibility, and never invest without thorough research.

Chapter 59: The Influencer Lie

How Influence Becomes Exploitation

You're scrolling through Instagram when a well-known influencer you admire shares a limited-time offer: **"Get luxury skincare products for 70% off using my special link!"** Eager to grab the deal, you follow the link and purchase the product. Days turn into weeks, and nothing arrives. You later discover the profile wasn't run by the influencer at all — it was a fraudster mimicking their account to promote scams.

This is the **Influencer Lie**, a tactic where scammers pose as influencers to exploit trust and social proof. By leveraging the perceived credibility and popularity of influencers, they trick victims into purchasing fake products, sharing personal details, or engaging with fraudulent services.

How It Works

1. **Impersonating an Influencer:** Fraudsters create fake profiles mimicking popular influencers or invent entirely new personas.

2. **Promoting Fake Deals:** They share posts or send direct messages offering exclusive discounts, giveaways, or investment opportunities.
3. **Exploiting Engagement:** Victims who follow the links are directed to fraudulent websites, where they lose money or share sensitive information.

The Influencer Lie succeeds because people associate influencers with trustworthiness and authentic recommendations.

Real-Life Examples

1. **Exclusive Collaboration Scams:** Fake influencers claim to launch limited-edition products, convincing followers to pre-order items that don't exist.
2. **Event Ticket Fraud:** Fraudsters impersonate influencers promoting "VIP access" to exclusive events, collecting payments for tickets that turn out to be fake.
3. **Personalized Advice Hoaxes:** Imposters offer one-on-one coaching or consultations for a fee, disappearing after receiving payment without providing the promised service.

Why It Works

The Influencer Lie preys on three psychological factors:

1. **Trust in Popularity:** People often trust influencers due to their large followings and perceived expertise.
2. **Desire for Deals:** Limited-time offers or exclusive discounts encourage impulsive decisions.
3. **Social Proof:** Comments and likes (often fake) make the promotion appear credible.

This tactic works because it combines the illusion of authenticity with urgency, prompting quick action.

How to Spot the Influencer Lie

1. **Check for Verification:** Genuine influencers often have verified accounts with a blue checkmark on platforms like Instagram or Twitter.
2. **Investigate Links:** Avoid clicking links from posts or profiles that seem suspicious or lack a clear connection to the influencer.

3. **Look for Interaction Patterns:** Fake influencer profiles often have inconsistent engagement, like lots of followers but very few likes or comments.

Exercise: Verify Influencer Promotions

1. Find a recent influencer post promoting a deal or product. Ask yourself:
   - "Is this post consistent with the influencer's usual content?"
   - "Does the link lead to the official website of the product or brand?"
2. Write down two ways to confirm the authenticity of influencer endorsements, such as cross-checking their website or contacting the brand directly.

Role-Playing Drill:

- Partner with someone. One person creates a fake influencer scenario, while the other practices identifying inconsistencies and verifying legitimacy.

Key Takeaway

The Influencer Lie manipulates trust in social media figures to promote scams. Always verify endorsements and check profiles for authenticity before engaging.

Chapter 60: The Phone App Fraud

When Convenience Comes at a Price

You're searching for a budgeting app and find one with excellent reviews and promises of easy-to-use features. You download it, enter your financial details to "track expenses," and think nothing of it. Weeks later, you notice unauthorized charges on your credit card. The app wasn't designed to help you manage money — it was created to steal it.

This is the **Phone App Fraud**, a tactic where scammers design fake apps that look legitimate but contain hidden malware or data-collection tools. By disguising malicious intent as helpful functionality, they gain access to sensitive information or exploit users financially.

How It Works

1. **Developing the App:** Scammers create apps that mimic popular tools, such as fitness trackers, budgeting software, or games.

2. **Uploading to App Stores:** These apps are uploaded to app stores, sometimes slipping past security reviews, or are promoted through third-party websites.
3. **Exploiting Users:** Once installed, the app collects sensitive data, such as passwords, or charges hidden fees for fake services.

The Phone App Fraud thrives on the convenience and ubiquity of mobile apps, making it easy to reach unsuspecting victims.

Real-Life Examples

1. **Fake Language Learning Apps:** Apps promising quick fluency in new languages collect sensitive data, such as email logins, during the registration process.
2. **Health Tracking Hoaxes:** Malicious apps claim to track steps or monitor sleep but secretly sell users' private health metrics to third parties.
3. **Gaming Add-On Scams:** Apps offering exclusive in-game content or cheats for popular games charge hidden fees or embed malware that compromises user devices.

Why It Works

The Phone App Fraud exploits three common behaviors:

1. **Trust in App Stores:** Many users assume all apps on official platforms such as Google Play or Apple's App Store are safe.
2. **Lack of Vigilance:** Most people don't thoroughly research apps before downloading, especially free ones.
3. **Convenience Over Security:** Victims prioritize features and ease of use, often overlooking potential risks.

This tactic works because it blends seamlessly into the routine of downloading and using mobile apps.

How to Spot the Phone App Fraud

1. **Check the Developer:** Verify the app's developer and ensure it's associated with a reputable company.
2. **Read Reviews Carefully:** Be cautious of apps with only glowing, generic reviews or very few downloads.

3. **Monitor Permissions:** Avoid apps that request unnecessary permissions, like access to your contacts or financial data.

Exercise: Evaluate a New App

1. Find an app you recently downloaded and ask yourself:
    - "Does this app's developer have a legitimate website?"
    - "Do the reviews include specific details, or are they oversimplistic?"
2. Write down two ways to verify app safety, such as researching the developer or checking for news about similar scams.

Role-Playing Drill:

- Partner with someone. One person presents a fake app scenario, while the other practices verifying the app's legitimacy before downloading.

Key Takeaway

The Phone App Fraud disguises malicious intent as helpful tools to exploit users. Always research apps, monitor permissions, and stick to downloads from reputable developers and app stores.

Section 4: Exploiting Cognitive Biases

Cognitive biases are mental shortcuts humans use to make decisions, but these shortcuts are far from fool proof. Manipulators exploit these biases to influence your choices without you realizing it. From your tendency to trust authority figures to your aversion to losses, these biases can be turned into tools for deception, steering your decisions in ways that serve someone else's agenda.

In this section, we'll expose how cognitive biases can be used against you and teach you to recognize and resist these manipulative tactics. By understanding how your mind works, you can protect yourself from being misled and regain control of your decision-making.

Chapter 61: The Authority Bias

When Authority Masks Intent

You receive a phone call from someone claiming to be from the IRS. The stern voice on the line warns: **"Your account is under review for tax evasion. If you don't pay $2,000 today, we'll issue an arrest warrant."** Terrified, you comply without questioning the legitimacy of the claim. Later, you discover the caller wasn't from the IRS — they used the Authority Bias to exploit your trust in official figures.

The **Authority Bias** is a cognitive shortcut where people defer to those they perceive as authoritative. Scammers manipulate this bias by mimicking authority figures to make their demands appear legitimate and unquestionable.

How It Works

1. **Adopting an Authoritative Persona:** Manipulators impersonate professionals such as government officials, or doctors.

2. **Creating Pressure:** They use formal language, official jargon, or dire consequences to make victims feel compelled to act immediately.
3. **Minimizing Doubts:** The appearance of authority discourages critical thinking, making people less likely to question the manipulator's claims.

The Authority Bias thrives on trust and the natural human tendency to respect those in perceived positions of power.

Real-Life Examples

1. **Legal Aid Scams:** Fraudsters claim to be attorneys, pressuring victims to pay "legal fees" for non-existent court cases.
2. **Academic Authority Fraud:** Manipulators pose as university representatives, demanding payments for fabricated tuition or exam-related issues.
3. **Inspection Hoaxes:** Scammers impersonate safety inspectors, pressuring businesses to pay fines for fake violations or buy unnecessary services.

Why It Works

The Authority Bias relies on three psychological triggers:

1. **Deference to Expertise:** People assume that authority figures have superior knowledge and rarely challenge their directives.
2. **Fear of Consequences:** Threats of punishment, fines, or other negative outcomes create a sense of urgency and compliance.
3. **Credibility Through Appearance:** Uniforms, titles, and formal language make manipulative claims seem legitimate.

This tactic works because it plays on deep-seated instincts to obey perceived authority.

How to Spot the Authority Bias

1. **Verify Credentials:** Always ask for identification or credentials and independently confirm their legitimacy.
2. **Beware of Urgency:** Legitimate authorities rarely pressure you to act immediately without verification.

3. **Question Unusual Requests:** Authority figures should not demand sensitive information or payments over the phone or online.

Exercise: Challenge Perceived Authority

1. Think of a recent situation where someone in authority influenced your decision. Reflect:
   - "Did I verify their identity before complying?"
   - "Did I feel pressured to act without questioning?"
2. Practice asking for credentials and taking time to verify claims in future interactions.

Role-Playing Drill:

- Partner with someone. One person acts as a manipulative authority figure, while the other practices questioning their legitimacy and verifying their claims.

Key Takeaway

The Authority Bias leverages trust in authority figures to manipulate decisions. Always verify credentials, question requests, and resist acting out of fear or urgency.

Chapter 62: The Recency Effect

How Recent Events Shape Choices

You're at a car dealership, debating whether to purchase the extended warranty. The salesperson leans in, saying: **"Just last week, a customer's transmission failed a month after their warranty expired — it cost them thousands to repair."** The story sticks in your mind, making you fear a similar fate. Convinced, you pay for the extended warranty, only to realize later that the decision was based on an isolated event rather than the actual reliability of the car.

This is the **Recency Effect**, a cognitive bias where recent information or events carry more weight in decision-making than they should. Manipulators exploit this bias by highlighting vivid, timely examples to sway choices, even when those examples don't represent the broader context.

How It Works

1. **Selecting the Example:** Manipulators choose a recent, memorable event or story that supports their agenda.

2. **Focusing Attention:** They emphasize the recency of the example, making it seem more relevant or probable than it actually is.
3. **Triggering Emotional Reactions:** The example is often framed to evoke strong emotions, like fear or urgency, to override rational thinking.

The Recency Effect succeeds because human memory is naturally biased toward recent events, making them seem more important than distant or less vivid examples.

Real-Life Examples

1. **Insurance Upselling:** Agents highlight recent accidents or disasters to convince customers to buy additional coverage, even when the risks are low.
2. **Media-Inspired Purchases:** After a news report about a food recall, customers may rush to buy organic or premium products, believing they're safer.
3. **Travel Fear Marketing:** Airlines or travel agencies promote "last-minute travel insurance" after a highly publicized travel mishap, using recent events to drive purchases.

Why It Works

The Recency Effect thrives on three factors:

1. **Emotional Impact:** Recent events feel more vivid and personal, especially if they evoke fear or loss.
2. **Ease of Recall:** Human memory prioritizes recent information, making it feel more relevant than older or abstract data.
3. **Sense of Urgency:** Recent examples create a perception that action must be taken immediately to avoid negative outcomes.

This tactic works because it avoids broader analysis, directing attention to one specific, timely detail.

How to Spot the Recency Effect

1. **Question the Context:** Ask whether the example reflects a broader trend or is an isolated incident.

2. **Look for Patterns:** Consider long-term data or historical information to balance recent anecdotes.
3. **Resist Emotional Triggers:** Be cautious when recent events are used to evoke fear, urgency, or other strong emotions.

Exercise: Challenge Recent Examples

1. Think of a recent decision influenced by a vivid story or event. Ask yourself:
   - "Was this example part of a pattern or a one-off occurrence?"
   - "What does the broader data suggest about this situation?"
2. Write down three questions to help evaluate future examples, such as:
   - "How representative is this event?"
   - "What are the odds of this happening to me?"

Role-Playing Drill:

- Partner with someone. One person presents a decision scenario based on a recent event, while the other practices identifying the Recency Effect and asking clarifying questions.

Key Takeaway

The Recency Effect uses recent events to distort decision-making. Balance timely examples with broader context and resist emotional responses to avoid being manipulated.

Chapter 63: The Commitment Trap

How Small Yeses Lead to Bigger Ones

At a mall, a fundraiser asks if you have a moment to discuss saving endangered animals. Feeling polite, you agree and listen to their pitch. Afterward, they ask if you'd like to make a small, one-time donation. You give $5, but before you leave, they suggest you sign up for a monthly donation plan. Because you've already said yes, it feels awkward to decline. Months later, you're still paying for a commitment you didn't intend to make.

This is the **Commitment Trap**, where manipulators use a series of escalating requests to exploit your desire for consistency. By securing a small initial agreement, they make it psychologically harder for you to say no to larger demands.

How It Works

1. **Starting Small:** Manipulators begin with a low-effort request, like signing a petition or answering a question, to build engagement.
2. **Escalating the Ask:** Once the victim agrees, they make a larger request that feels consistent with the initial commitment.
3. **Leveraging Cognitive Dissonance:** Saying no after an initial yes feels inconsistent, creating discomfort that leads victims to comply.

The Commitment Trap works because humans have a natural tendency to stay consistent with their previous actions and statements.

Real-Life Examples

1. **Sales Techniques:** Car dealers get customers to agree to small add-ons before suggesting costly upgrades or warranties.
2. **Fundraising Campaigns:** Charities ask for small donations first, later pushing for recurring contributions or larger gifts.
3. **Online Free Trials:** Free trials hook users into paid subscriptions by requiring small actions, like entering credit card details.

Why It Works

The Commitment Trap thrives on three psychological tendencies:

1. **Desire for Consistency:** People want to appear consistent in their actions and decisions.
2. **Escalation of Investment:** Each additional commitment makes backing out feel more difficult.
3. **Social Pressure:** Manipulators frame the larger request as a natural next step, making refusal seem unreasonable.

This tactic works because it turns politeness and small actions into gateways for larger obligations.

How to Spot the Commitment Trap

1. **Recognize the Pattern:** Be cautious when a small agreement is quickly followed by a larger request.
2. **Pause Before Escalating:** Reflect on whether the larger commitment aligns with your actual goals or intentions.
3. **Separate Decisions:** Treat each request as a standalone decision, not an extension of previous actions.

Exercise: Reflect on Past Commitments

1. Think of a time you agreed to something small but felt pressured to escalate. Ask yourself:
   - "Did I feel obligated to say yes because of my earlier action?"
   - "Would I have agreed to the larger request if it came first?"
2. Write down two strategies to pause and evaluate larger requests in the future.

Role-Playing Drill:

- Partner with someone. One person presents a small, harmless request, escalating it into a larger one. The other practices recognizing the trap and declining without guilt.

Key Takeaway

The Commitment Trap turns small agreements into larger obligations. Stay mindful of escalating requests, and remember: you're not obligated to say yes just to stay consistent.

Chapter 64: The Consensus Effect

How Popularity Becomes Persuasion

You're browsing an online store and see a product with hundreds of five-star reviews and testimonials claiming, **"This is the best purchase I've ever made!"** Trusting the overwhelming positivity, you buy it. When it arrives, it's poorly made and doesn't match the description. Frustrated, you revisit the site and realize many of the reviews are suspiciously similar, and the reviewers don't seem legitimate.

This is the **Consensus Effect**, a tactic where manipulators create the illusion of widespread approval to sway decisions. By fabricating popularity, they make their product, service, or message seem trustworthy and desirable.

How It Works

1. **Generating Fake Support:** Manipulators write or pay for fake reviews, likes, or endorsements to create the appearance of popularity.

2. **Exploiting Social Proof:** People tend to trust and follow the crowd, assuming popular choices are the safest or best.
3. **Minimizing Doubts:** High ratings or glowing testimonials discourage critical thinking or further research.

The Consensus Effect thrives because humans often trust collective judgment, especially when making quick decisions.

Real-Life Examples

1. **Fake Product Reviews:** Online sellers inflate ratings and reviews to make low-quality items appear reliable.
2. **Social Media Endorsements:** Fraudsters buy fake followers and likes to appear influential, convincing people to trust them.
3. **Event Popularity Scams:** Manipulators falsely claim that events are "sold out" or highly attended to drive ticket sales.

Why It Works

The Consensus Effect relies on three psychological tendencies:

1. **Trust in Numbers:** People assume large groups can't be wrong, so popularity is equated with quality or legitimacy.
2. **Perceived Demand:** High popularity makes people believe the product or service is highly sought-after, prompting quick decisions to avoid losing an opportunity.
3. **Reduced Scrutiny:** Widespread approval discourages people from questioning the details.

This tactic works because it creates a false sense of security by leveraging social validation.

How to Spot the Consensus Effect

1. **Check Reviewer Patterns:** Look for signs of fake reviews, such as generic language, similar usernames, or identical posting times.

2. **Verify Social Proof:** Investigate whether endorsements or high ratings come from credible sources.
3. **Don't Be Fooled By Overwhelming Positivity:** Products or services with only glowing feedback may be too good to be true.

Exercise: Investigate Social Proof

1. Choose a product or service with high ratings and ask yourself:
   - "Are these reviews specific and credible?"
   - "Do the reviewers have a history of authentic activity?"
2. Write down two methods to verify the legitimacy of popularity claims, such as cross-checking reviews on multiple platforms.

Role-Playing Drill:

- Partner with someone. One person creates a scenario involving fake social proof, while the other practices identifying red flags and verifying authenticity.

Key Takeaway

The Consensus Effect manipulates trust in popularity to influence decisions. Always investigate reviews, endorsements, and ratings to ensure they're legitimate before acting.

Chapter 65: The Rarity Mirage

When Scarcity Turns into Deception

You're browsing a travel website for vacation deals. One offer catches your attention: **"3 seats left at this price!"** Concerned about missing the deal, you immediately book your ticket. Days later, you revisit the same site, only to find the exact same deal with the same warning. You realize the scarcity message was fake, designed to rush you into making a decision.

This is the **Rarity Mirage**, a tactic where manipulators fabricate scarcity to make products or opportunities seem more valuable. By convincing you something is in short supply, they trigger an emotional response that overrides logical decision-making.

How It Works

1. **Creating False Limits:** Manipulators display fake low-stock warnings, like "Last Few in Stock" or "Exclusive Item."

2. **Inflating Urgency with Timers:** They use countdown clocks to suggest fleeting opportunities, pushing for rushed decisions.
3. **Amplifying Exclusivity:** The item is marketed as rare or unavailable elsewhere, increasing its perceived worth.

The Rarity Mirage is effective because humans are psychologically programmed to value things that appear scarce, associating rarity with importance or desirability.

Real-Life Examples

1. **Fake Hotel Bookings:** Travel websites display alerts like "3 people are looking at this room," even when no one else is browsing.
2. **Online Auctions:** Sellers create fake bidding wars to inflate prices, making buyers believe the item is highly sought after.
3. **Streaming Service Hype:** Limited-time access to shows or events prompts viewers to subscribe or renew memberships unnecessarily.

Why It Works

The Rarity Mirage capitalizes on three psychological triggers:

1. **Value Through Scarcity:** People associate rarity with higher value or exclusivity.
2. **Fear of Losing Out On a Deal:** The possibility of missing a "one-time" opportunity creates anxiety and urgency.
3. **Impulsive Decision-Making:** Scarcity disrupts logical evaluation, prompting immediate action.

This tactic works because it overrides careful consideration with emotional urgency.

How to Spot the Rarity Mirage

1. **Refresh the Website Page You Are Visiting:** Fake scarcity tactics often reset when you reload the website.
2. **Research Availability:** Check whether the same item is sold elsewhere or if similar deals are offered by competitors.
3. **Pause Before Acting:** Resist the urge to buy immediately — most "limited offers" don't truly expire.

Exercise: Test Scarcity Claims

1. Visit an online store with low-stock warnings. Ask yourself:
    - "Does the warning change if I refresh or return later?"
    - "Is this product available from other retailers?"
2. Write down two strategies to resist scarcity pressure, such as waiting 24 hours before making a purchase.

Role-Playing Drill:

- Partner with someone. One person creates a scarcity scenario, while the other practices identifying manipulation and staying calm under pressure.

Key Takeaway

The Rarity Mirage manipulates urgency and scarcity to pressure decisions. Always verify claims of limited availability and avoid rushing purchases driven by fear of missing out.

Chapter 66: The Extreme Evaluator

I got the $2,500 TV — it seemed like a good deal compared to the $5,000 one.
But was it more than you wanted to spend in the first place?

How Comparisons Shape Decisions

You're shopping for a new TV, and the salesperson shows you a $5,000 state-of-the-art model. Shocked at the price, you immediately decline. Then they show you another option, priced at $2,500, emphasizing it has most of the same features. Relieved by the contrast, you purchase it, even though it's still more expensive than you planned to spend.

This is the **Extreme Evaluator**, a tactic where manipulators use extreme comparisons to influence decisions. By presenting an exaggerated option first, they make the alternative seem more reasonable, even if it's still overpriced or unnecessary.

How It Works

1. **Introducing an Outlier:** Manipulators begin with an exaggerated or impractical option to make the next choice seem more appealing.

2. **Positioning a Preferred Choice:** They strategically highlight an alternative that appears balanced or favorable in comparison to the extreme option.
3. **Leveraging Relative Value:** The contrast between the options shifts focus away from the actual cost or relevance of the preferred choice.

The Extreme Evaluator is effective because human decision-making is heavily influenced by context, making comparisons a powerful tool for shaping perceptions.

Real-Life Examples

1. **Upselling at Restaurants:** Menus include a $150 steak to make the $75 steak seem affordable, even though both are overpriced.
2. **Gym Memberships:** Gyms show premium packages with high fees to make the mid-tier package look like better value.
3. **Tech Gadgets:** Retailers display overpriced flagship products to push customers toward mid-range models with higher profit margins.

How to Spot the Extreme Evaluator

1. **Revisit Your Original Needs:** Before comparing options, ask if the alternatives meet your initial goals or budget.
2. **Question the Context:** Be wary when the first option is excessively high or seems out of place — it may be there to influence your perception.
3. **Research Alternatives Independently:** Check if similar products or services are available at better prices elsewhere.

Exercise: Reflect on Past Purchases

1. Think of a time you chose an option because it seemed reasonable compared to a more expensive alternative. Reflect:
   - "Would I have chosen this if the first option hadn't been presented?"
   - "Did I spend more than I originally planned?"

Role-Playing Drill:

- Partner with someone. One person presents an exaggerated option, followed by a more "reasonable" one. The other practices identifying the tactic and focusing on their original budget or needs.

Key Takeaway

The Extreme Evaluator manipulates your choices by setting unrealistic comparisons to influence your perception of value. Always review options based on your needs, not on the contrast presented to you.

Chapter 67: The Availability Heuristic

How Recent Events Cloud Judgment

You're planning a vacation to a coastal city when a news report flashes: **"Shark Attack Claims Life of Swimmer."** The story sticks in your mind, and you cancel your trip, choosing a mountain destination instead. What you don't realize is that shark attacks are incredibly rare, but the vividness of the story made it feel like a likely risk.

This is the **Availability Heuristic**, a cognitive bias where recent or vivid examples dominate your decision-making. Manipulators use this bias by highlighting specific events or anecdotes that distort your perception of reality, making improbable risks seem imminent.

How It Works

1. **Highlighting Memorable Events:** Manipulators emphasize unusual, vivid examples to influence your choices.

2. **Skewing Risk Perception:** By focusing on a specific event, they make it seem more common or probable than it actually is.
3. **Triggering Emotional Reactions:** The vividness of the example clouds logical evaluation of actual risks.

The Availability Heuristic works because the human brain prioritizes information that is easy to recall, even if it's not representative of broader trends.

Real-Life Examples

1. **Travel Safety Concerns:** Highlighting a recent plane crash causes travelers to overestimate the danger of flying.
2. **Health Product Marketing:** Ads show dramatic testimonials of miraculous recoveries to sell supplements, even if such cases are rare.
3. **Home Security Sales:** Burglary anecdotes from neighboring towns are used to convince homeowners to install expensive security systems.

How to Spot the Availability Heuristic

1. **Question the Sample Size:** Ask if the example reflects a broader trend or is an isolated incident.
2. **Research the Actual Risk:** Look for statistics or data to validate the likelihood of the event influencing your decision.
3. **Resist Emotional Reactions:** Be cautious of decisions driven by fear, excitement, or other strong emotions tied to specific examples.

Exercise: Test Vivid Examples

1. Recall a recent decision influenced by a vivid example. Ask yourself:
    - "Was this event likely, or was it memorable because it was unusual?"
    - "Did I consider other possibilities or just focus on this one example?"

Role-Playing Drill:

- Partner with someone. One person presents a vivid anecdote to influence a decision, while the other practices questioning its relevance and considering broader context.

Key Takeaway

The Availability Heuristic uses vivid or recent examples to distort your judgment of likelihood or risk. Balance anecdotal examples with statistical data to make more informed decisions.

Chapter 68: The Familiarity Bias

When Familiarity Breeds Trust

You're planning a family vacation and searching for a travel agency. One agency catches your attention because you've seen their ads on Instagram, YouTube, and even in magazines. Their tagline, **"Trusted by millions,"** sticks in your mind. Without comparing alternatives, you book a package through them, assuming their widespread presence means reliability. After the trip, you realize you overpaid and that better deals were available through lesser-known providers.

This is the **Familiarity Bias**, where repeated exposure creates a sense of trust or credibility. Manipulators exploit this bias by flooding your attention with consistent messaging, making you believe their service or product is the best option without evidence to back it up.

How It Works

1. **Flooding the Audience:** Manipulators ensure their brand, product, or idea appears in multiple places — ads, emails, social media, or word-of-mouth.

2. **Creating a Sense of Comfort:** Familiar messages make people feel at ease, leading them to perceive them as safe or credible.
3. **Lowering Critical Evaluation:** Repeated exposure makes people less likely to question the validity of the product or idea, as familiarity creates an illusion of trustworthiness.

The Familiarity Bias works because humans instinctively trust what they recognize, associating these messages with safety and legitimacy.

Real-Life Examples

1. **Streaming Platforms:** A new series is repeatedly advertised across social media, email newsletters, and app notifications, making viewers assume it's a must-watch hit.
2. **Job Recruitment Services:** Career platforms constantly show the same companies in job recommendations, leading job seekers to perceive them as top employers without checking reviews.
3. **Charity Campaigns:** Non-profits bombard potential donors with the same message across mailers, emails, and ads, fostering trust through repeated exposure rather than transparent credibility.

Why It Works

The Familiarity Bias relies on three key tendencies:

1. **Comfort in Recognition:** People feel safer with things they've encountered multiple times, even if they're unfamiliar with the details.
2. **Shortcut to Credibility:** Familiarity creates the illusion of legitimacy, saving the brain from deeper analysis.
3. **Reduced Suspicion:** Overexposure dulls doubt, making the subject seem less like a risk.

This tactic works because it plays on the human tendency to associate repeating statements with trustworthiness.

How to Spot the Familiarity Bias

1. **Check the Source:** Ensure the subject's credibility by researching its background and legitimacy, not just its visibility.
2. **Look Beyond the Surface:** Compare alternatives before deciding.
3. **Notice Patterns:** Be wary when the same messages or claims appear frequently without substantive proof.

Exercise: Analyze Repeated Messages

1. Think of a brand or product you've seen advertised repeatedly. Ask yourself:
   - "What specific evidence supports their claims?"
   - "Have I considered other options, or am I choosing them because they're familiar?"
2. Write down two steps you can take to verify credibility beyond repeated exposure, such as checking reviews or independent sources.

Role-Playing Drill:

- Partner with someone. One person presents a product with repeated messaging, while the other practices asking questions to assess its legitimacy.

Key Takeaway

The Familiarity Bias manipulates trust through repeating messages, making something appear reliable without actual proof. Always verify credibility beyond repeated exposure and consider alternatives before committing.

Chapter 69: The Framing Effect

How Presentation Changes Decisions

You're offered a payment plan for a subscription service. The representative presents two options: **"Pay $500 annually upfront"** or **"Only $45 a month for unlimited access!"** You choose the monthly option, feeling it's a better deal, even though it costs $540 over the year. The way the information was framed influenced your perception of value.

This is the **Framing Effect**, where the way information is presented shapes how it's perceived. Manipulators exploit this bias by emphasizing positive aspects or downplaying negatives, steering decisions toward their desired outcome.

How It Works

1. **Emphasizing Positives:** Manipulators highlight favorable details, such as discounts or bonuses, while minimizing drawbacks.
2. **Strategic Language Choices:** The use of words like "only" or "exclusive" influences how information is interpreted.

3. **Hiding True Costs:** Information is framed to make expenses or risks seem smaller or less significant.

The Framing Effect works because humans rely on context and presentation to evaluate choices, often making snap judgments based on surface impressions.

Real-Life Examples

1. **Medical Decisions:** A treatment is described as having a 90% success rate instead of a 10% failure rate, making it sound more appealing.
2. **Restaurant Menus:** Items are labeled as "Chef's Special" or "Locally Sourced" to frame them as premium, justifying higher prices.
3. **Retail Discounts:** Stores highlight **"You save $50!"** instead of simply listing the price, focusing attention on perceived value.

Why It Works

The Framing Effect thrives on three psychological factors:

1. **Context Drives Perception:** People interpret information differently depending on how it's presented.
2. **Positive Over Negative Framing:** Humans are naturally drawn to benefits and tend to avoid focusing on losses or risks.
3. **Reduced Analytical Thinking:** Framing shortcuts logical evaluation, making surface impressions more influential.

This tactic works because it leverages presentation to guide interpretation, often without the victim noticing.

How to Spot the Framing Effect

1. **Rephrase the Information:** Reframe the details yourself to see how the context changes your perception.
2. **Focus on the Facts:** Look beyond how something is presented and evaluate the core details objectively.
3. **Compare Alternatives:** Consider how similar options are described to detect manipulative framing.

Exercise: Reframe a Scenario

1. Think of a recent decision influenced by framing. Ask yourself:
    - "How would I perceive this if it were presented differently?"
    - "Does the framing align with the actual value or cost?"
2. Practice rephrasing offers or descriptions to uncover their true meaning.

Role-Playing Drill:

- Partner with someone. One person presents a framed scenario, while the other practices rephrasing it to evaluate the decision objectively.

Key Takeaway

The Framing Effect shapes decisions by manipulating how information is presented. Stay focused on the facts and reframe details to see the full picture before making choices.

Chapter 70: The Halo Effect

When Positivity Overshadows the Truth

You're shopping for a new smartphone and are drawn to a specific brand known for its sleek design. The salesperson praises the device's aesthetics, emphasizing its elegant build and premium look. Impressed, you purchase it without thoroughly comparing features or researching reviews. Later, you discover the phone's performance and battery life don't match its high price.

This is the **Halo Effect**, where a single positive trait, like appearance or reputation, leads to an inflated perception of overall quality. Manipulators exploit this bias by focusing on one standout feature to distract from flaws or shortcomings.

How It Works

1. **Highlighting Strengths:** Manipulators emphasize a single positive attribute, like visual appeal or past success, to influence perception.

2. **Creating Emotional Appeal:** They use that strength to evoke admiration, trust, or excitement, diverting attention from potential negatives.
3. **Leveraging Assumptions:** Victims assume that excellence in one area reflects the overall quality, even when there's no evidence to support it.

The Halo Effect works because humans often generalize, letting a single positive aspect dominate their evaluation.

Real-Life Examples

1. **Celebrity Endorsements:** A famous athlete promotes a sports drink, leading people to assume it's the healthiest option despite lacking nutritional proof.
2. **Corporate Reputation:** A company with a strong environmental record launches a product, and customers assume it's high-quality without further research.
3. **Luxury Branding:** A high-end clothing brand known for its stylish designs launches a line of accessories. Customers assume the accessories are equally high-quality, even though they haven't been reviewed or tested.

Why It Works

The Halo Effect relies on three cognitive tendencies:

1. **Attraction to Excellence:** People are drawn to outstanding traits and often associate them with overall quality.
2. **Mental Shortcuts:** The brain simplifies evaluations by generalizing from one positive aspect.
3. **Reduced Doubt:** Admiration for a standout trait lowers critical analysis of other factors.

This tactic works because it builds trust and credibility through partial impressions rather than complete assessments.

How to Spot the Halo Effect

1. **Look Beyond the Highlight:** Ask whether the emphasized trait truly reflects the overall quality of the product, person, or service.
2. **Research Details:** Investigate other features or aspects that may have been overshadowed.
3. **Question Assumptions:** Challenge whether the positive trait is relevant to your decision or merely a distraction.

Exercise: Identify a Halo Bias

1. Think of a recent purchase influenced by one standout feature. Reflect:
    - "Did this feature align with the overall quality?"
    - "Were there other factors I overlooked?"
2. Write down two ways to evaluate items holistically in the future, such as comparing multiple features or checking reviews.

Role-Playing Drill:

- Partner with someone. One person highlights a single exceptional trait of a product or service, while the other practices identifying and questioning potential shortcomings.

Key Takeaway

The Halo Effect leverages a single positive trait to create unwarranted trust. Always evaluate all aspects of a decision and avoid letting one strength overshadow critical thinking.

Chapter 71: The Dunning-Kruger Effect Exploit

How Overconfidence Becomes a Tool for Manipulation

Imagine you're at a seminar on stock trading. The presenter teaches basic concepts like "buy low, sell high," praising the audience for their quick understanding. Feeling empowered, you purchase their advanced course and software tools, believing you're ready to become a professional trader. Weeks later, you realize you've spent hundreds of dollars but lack the deeper expertise needed for success.

This is the **Dunning-Kruger Effect Exploit**, where manipulators convince people they've mastered a topic after gaining minimal knowledge. By inflating confidence, they prompt individuals to make risky decisions, often to the manipulator's advantage.

How It Works

1. **Simplifying Concepts:** Manipulators present basic information as ground-breaking knowledge to make victims feel competent.
2. **Praising Quick Learners:** They exaggerate the victim's progress, building a false sense of expertise.
3. **Encouraging Overreach:** Once victims feel overconfident, manipulators push them to make larger commitments, like investments or purchases.

This tactic works because humans tend to overestimate their abilities after learning the basics of a subject, believing they're more skilled than they truly are.

Real-Life Examples

1. **Get-Rich-Quick Schemes:** Scammers teach simplistic financial strategies, convincing victims they can achieve wealth easily if they buy expensive resources.
2. **Fitness Plans:** Manipulators overpraise beginners for basic workouts, selling them advanced training programs they're not ready for.
3. **DIY Tutorials:** Minimal knowledge from tutorials is framed as sufficient expertise, encouraging people to buy expensive tools or materials for complex projects.

Why It Works

The Dunning-Kruger Effect Exploit thrives on three psychological tendencies:

1. **Overestimation of Knowledge:** People with limited knowledge often believe they know more than they actually do.
2. **Desire for Mastery:** Victims want to feel competent, making them receptive to flattery and praise.
3. **Ignoring Complexity:** Simplistic explanations create the illusion that a subject is easy to master, reducing caution.

This tactic works because it feeds overconfidence, pushing victims into decisions they're not prepared to make.

How to Spot the Dunning-Kruger Effect Exploit

1. **Assess the Complexity:** Ask yourself if the topic is being oversimplified or if there's more to learn.
2. **Seek Third-Party Validation:** Research whether the claims being made align with expert opinions or credible sources.
3. **Pause Before Committing:** Reflect on whether your confidence matches your actual level of understanding.

Exercise: Test Your Knowledge

1. Think of a subject where you feel confident after learning the basics. Ask yourself:
   - "How would an expert view my understanding?"
   - "What areas of this topic do I still need to explore?"
2. Write down two ways to assess your expertise more accurately, such as consulting a professional or diving deeper into advanced resources.

Role-Playing Drill:

- Partner with someone. One person presents a simplified scenario, while the other practices identifying gaps in their understanding and resisting overconfidence.

Key Takeaway

The Dunning-Kruger Effect Exploit inflates confidence to manipulate decisions. Recognize the limits of your knowledge, seek credible sources, and avoid acting on premature confidence.

Chapter 72: The Single Trait Trap

How One Trait Dominates the Decision

You're shopping for a new car, and the salesperson highlights its incredible fuel efficiency, claiming it will save you money in the long run. The advertisements also showcase glowing testimonials about the car's low gas consumption. Convinced, you make the purchase, but later you realize the car lacks important safety features and has expensive maintenance costs.

This is the **Single Trait Trap**, where one standout feature is exaggerated to divert attention from flaws or risks. Manipulators rely on this tactic to steer decisions, knowing that focusing on a single appealing trait will prevent a more thorough evaluation.

How It Works

1. **Highlighting the Strength:** Manipulators focus on a standout feature or benefit, ignoring potential downsides.

2. **Reinforcing the Message:** They repeat the positive trait in marketing, sales pitches, or reviews to make it the focal point.
3. **Downplaying Negatives:** Flaws are omitted, minimized, or hidden, ensuring the emphasis remains on the chosen characteristic.

The Single Trait Trap works because people naturally focus on memorable or impressive details, often neglecting a broader analysis.

Real-Life Examples

1. **Luxury Branding:** A watch brand markets its "Swiss craftsmanship" while concealing its high repair costs and lack of durability.
2. **Job Candidate Evaluations:** A candidate's prestigious university degree overshadows their lack of relevant experience.
3. **Real Estate Sales:** A house with a beautiful backyard is promoted heavily, while structural issues or poor location are downplayed.

Why It Works

The Single Trait Trap thrives on three psychological tendencies:

1. **Focus on Excellence:** People are drawn to standout qualities and often assume they indicate overall value.
2. **Limited Attention Span:** It's easier to focus on one striking feature than to evaluate a product or situation holistically.
3. **Emotional Anchoring:** A single positive trait creates a sense of trust or desire, reducing doubt about other aspects.

This tactic works because it narrows attention to one appealing characteristic, making it harder to consider other factors.

How to Spot the Single Trait Trap

1. **Identify Missing Information:** Ask whether other important details are being ignored or hidden.

2. **Balance Features:** Evaluate how the standout trait compares to other essential factors for your decision.
3. **Seek Unbiased Reviews:** Look for feedback that considers both strengths and weaknesses.

Exercise: Evaluate a Single Trait

1. Think of a product or service you were drawn to because of one specific feature. Ask yourself:
    - "Did I overlook other factors?"
    - "Would I make the same decision if I focused on the full picture?"
2. Practice identifying other critical traits or areas for future evaluations.

Role-Playing Drill:

- Partner with someone. One person emphasizes a single positive trait in a product or scenario, while the other practices asking about additional details and potential downsides.

Key Takeaway

The Single Trait Trap manipulates focus by emphasizing one positive characteristic while hiding flaws. Always evaluate the full picture and question whether other factors are being intentionally downplayed.

Chapter 73: The Loss Aversion Conundrum

When Fear of Loss Drives Decisions

You're considering joining a fitness program but feel unsure about the cost. The trainer emails you, saying, **"If you don't sign up by midnight, you'll miss out on this $150 discount."** The thought of losing the deal pushes you to enroll immediately, even though you're not completely confident it's the right fit.

This is the **Loss Aversion Conundrum**, a tactic where manipulators highlight what you'll lose by not acting rather than what you might gain. By focusing on potential losses, they trigger a psychological response that prioritizes avoiding regret over logical decision-making.

How It Works

1. **Highlighting Missed Opportunities:** Manipulators frame decisions around what victims could lose rather than potential benefits.

2. **Creating Emotional Pressure:** The fear of missing out on value or opportunity drives impulsive actions.
3. **Minimizing Rational Analysis:** Victims focus on avoiding immediate loss, often neglecting to evaluate long-term outcomes.

The Loss Aversion Conundrum works because humans feel the pain of loss more acutely than the pleasure of gain, making loss avoidance a powerful motivator.

Real-Life Examples

1. **Exclusive Event Invitations:** Organizers claim tickets are selling out quickly, pressuring attendees to book immediately, even though plenty of seats remain available.
2. **Auto Warranty Notices:** Car warranty companies send letters stating coverage will "end soon," encouraging unnecessary renewals or upgrades.
3. **Loyalty Program Alerts:** Retailers warn customers that accumulated rewards points will expire shortly, prompting rushed purchases to redeem them.

Why It Works

The Loss Aversion Conundrum leverages three psychological tendencies:

1. **Pain of Loss:** People often feel more motivated to avoid losing something they already have than to gain something new.
2. **Urgency to Act:** The thought of losing out creates a sense of immediate pressure, leading to snap decisions.
3. **Emotional Weight:** Loss carries a heavier emotional impact than equivalent gains, making it a stronger motivator.

This tactic works because it turns potential loss into a priority, often overriding logical evaluation.

How to Spot the Loss Aversion Conundrum

1. **Identify the Framing:** Ask whether the offer focuses on what you're losing instead of what you're gaining.

2. **Pause to Evaluate:** Step back and consider if the urgency is genuine or manufactured.
3. **Compare Long-Term Impact:** Reflect on whether acting quickly aligns with your overall goals or priorities.

Exercise: Reflect on Loss Framing

1. Think of a recent decision driven by a fear of loss. Ask yourself:
    - "Was the urgency real, or was it created to pressure me?"
    - "Did I consider the benefits and risks equally?"
2. Write down two strategies to avoid being pressured by loss-focused messaging, such as setting a 24-hour pause rule.

Role-Playing Drill:

- Partner with someone. One person uses loss aversion messaging to create urgency, while the other practices identifying the tactic and evaluating the decision objectively.

Key Takeaway

The Loss Aversion Conundrum manipulates decisions by focusing on potential losses. Avoid rushing into actions — evaluate both risks and rewards before deciding.

Chapter 74: The Status Quo Bias Manipulation

When Comfort Leads to Missed Opportunities

You've had the same Internet provider for years, despite frequent outages and rising costs. Every time you consider switching, the thought of researching alternatives and going through the process feels overwhelming. The provider sends you a loyalty discount to encourage you to stay, and you renew your plan without exploring better options.

This is the **Status Quo Bias Manipulation**, where manipulators rely on the human tendency to stick with familiar choices rather than explore new ones. By making change seem inconvenient or unnecessary, they maintain control over your decisions.

How It Works

1. **Reinforcing Familiarity:** Manipulators emphasize the comfort and reliability of the current option.

2. **Highlighting Effort:** They exaggerate the effort or risk involved in making a change.
3. **Framing Alternatives as Uncertain:** New options are portrayed as risky or unreliable, discouraging exploration.

The Status Quo Bias Manipulation works because humans naturally prefer stability and consistency, even when change could lead to better outcomes.

Real-Life Examples

1. **Utility Providers:** Electricity or cable companies offer small loyalty discounts to keep customers from switching to cheaper competitors.
2. **Banking Services:** Banks stress the "seamlessness" of staying with their accounts while downplaying the benefits of moving to another institution.
3. **Corporate Software:** Businesses discourage switching platforms by emphasizing the costs of training employees on new systems.

Why It Works

This manipulation relies on three psychological tendencies:

1. **Comfort in Familiarity:** People prefer sticking with what they know rather than taking risks with the unknown.
2. **Avoidance of Effort:** Change often requires time, research, and adjustments, which many people instinctively avoid.
3. **Perception of Stability:** Familiar options are perceived as safer and less likely to disrupt existing routines.

This tactic works because it keeps people locked into decisions by making alternatives seem unappealing or overly complex.

How to Spot the Status Quo Bias Manipulation

1. **Evaluate Alternatives:** Take the time to explore and compare other options, even if they require effort.
2. **Recognize Emotional Barriers:** Identify whether hesitation comes from fear of disruption or actual risks.

3. **Weigh Long-Term Benefits:** Consider whether staying with the familiar truly serves your best interests.

Exercise: Challenge Your Comfort Zone

1. Think of a service, subscription, or routine you've stuck with for years. Reflect:
   - "Have I actively compared alternatives?"
   - "What benefits might I gain from exploring new options?"
2. Write down two steps you can take to evaluate alternatives, such as researching reviews or seeking recommendations.

Role-Playing Drill:

- Partner with someone. One person plays the role of a service provider emphasizing the ease of staying, while the other practices weighing pros and cons of switching.

Key Takeaway

The Status Quo Bias Manipulation uses comfort and familiarity to maintain control over your decisions. Take the time to evaluate whether staying in your current situation truly aligns with your goals or if change could benefit you.

Chapter 75: The Optimism Bias Trick

When Optimism Clouds Judgment

You're offered a discounted extended warranty for a laptop. Confident in its brand reputation and your careful handling, you decline, thinking, **"I've never needed a warranty before."** A few months later, the laptop unexpectedly malfunctions, and the repair costs outweigh the original price of the warranty.

This is the **Optimism Bias Trick**, where manipulators exploit the assumption that bad outcomes are unlikely to happen to you. By reinforcing overconfidence and minimizing risks, they prompt decisions that ignore potential downsides.

How It Works

1. **Minimizing Risk Perception:** Manipulators reassure you that the likelihood of problems is slim or irrelevant.
2. **Encouraging Overconfidence:** They appeal to your belief in your own good luck, skills, or judgment to downplay caution.

3. **Redirecting Focus:** By emphasizing benefits or positive possibilities, they shift attention away from safeguards or contingencies.

The Optimism Bias Trick works because humans often overestimate their immunity to negative outcomes, leading to riskier choices.

Real-Life Examples

1. **Travel Insurance Declines:** Agents subtly encourage travelers to skip insurance, framing it as unnecessary for their "safe" plans.
2. **Loan Agreements:** Borrowers are encouraged to take on high-interest loans, assuming they'll repay quickly without considering financial challenges.
3. **Event Deposits:** Companies emphasize non-refundable terms after assuring customers that cancellations are unlikely.

Why It Works

This manipulation relies on three cognitive tendencies:

1. **Overestimation of Personal Control:** People believe their actions or decisions will prevent bad outcomes.
2. **Focus on Positive Scenarios:** Optimism narrows attention to best-case outcomes, ignoring potential risks.
3. **Aversion to Planning for Problems:** Preparing for potential setbacks feels unnecessary when outcomes seem assured.

This tactic works because it reinforces confidence, reducing precautionary measures or thorough evaluation.

How to Spot the Optimism Bias Trick

1. **Consider Past Experiences:** Reflect on whether previous decisions turned out differently than expected.
2. **Anticipate Worst-Case Scenarios:** Ask, "What would I do if things didn't go as planned?"
3. **Research Alternatives:** Look for unbiased opinions or data that highlight risks or precautions.

Exercise: Reflect on Missed Precautions

1. Think of a recent decision where optimism influenced your choice. Reflect:
   - "What risks did I overlook?"
   - "How could I have prepared better?"
2. Write down two steps to ensure balanced decision-making, such as researching risks or consulting experts.

Role-Playing Drill:

- Partner with someone. One person presents an overly optimistic scenario, while the other practices identifying potential risks and countermeasures.

Key Takeaway

The Optimism Bias Trick manipulates your confidence, making you overlook risks and safeguards. Balance positive expectations with realistic preparation to avoid unexpected setbacks.

Chapter 76: The Confirmation Bias Bait

How Familiar Ideas Build Trust

You're considering a new fitness program and come across an ad that says, **"Scientific evidence proves that high-intensity workouts burn more calories."** Since you already believe high-intensity workouts are effective, you quickly sign up for the program without exploring other options. Later, you discover the plan doesn't align with your fitness goals or health needs.

This is the **Confirmation Bias Bait**, a tactic where manipulators provide information that aligns with your existing beliefs to gain trust and steer your decisions. By confirming what you already think is true, they bypass critical analysis and guide you into their desired outcome.

How It Works

1. **Identifying Beliefs:** Manipulators study your preferences, opinions, or biases to craft targeted messages.

2. **Reinforcing Comfort Zones:** They provide data, testimonials, or stories that align with your existing worldview, making their offer seem trustworthy.
3. **Suppressing Contradictory Evidence:** Dissenting information is omitted, keeping you focused on their carefully curated narrative.

The Confirmation Bias Bait works because humans naturally seek information that supports their beliefs and avoid details that challenge them.

Real-Life Examples

1. **Eco-Friendly Branding:** A cleaning product advertises its use of natural ingredients to appeal to environmentally conscious consumers, while omitting its high plastic packaging usage.
2. **Streaming Recommendations:** A platform promotes shows or movies that match a user's viewing history, encouraging continued subscriptions without showcasing diverse options.
3. **Education Programs:** Online courses emphasize how their teaching aligns with widely accepted study methods but neglect to mention the lack of accreditation or credentials.

Why It Works

This manipulation leverages three psychological tendencies:

1. **Comfort in Agreement:** People are more likely to trust information that aligns with their pre-existing beliefs.
2. **Selective Attention:** Victims focus on supportive details, ignoring gaps or alternative perspectives.
3. **Resistance to Contradiction:** Contradictory information feels uncomfortable, reducing motivation to seek it out.

This tactic works because it creates a false sense of validation, leading people to lower their guard.

How to Spot the Confirmation Bias Bait

1. **Seek Contrasting Perspectives:** Explore alternative viewpoints or information that challenges your assumptions.

2. **Check for Missing Details:** Ask whether important facts or counterarguments are being excluded.
3. **Verify Claims Independently:** Research the sources or data supporting the message to ensure accuracy.

Exercise: Test Your Assumptions

1. Identify a recent decision that aligned with your beliefs. Ask yourself:
   - "Did I actively seek out alternative viewpoints?"
   - "Was I presented with all the relevant information?"
2. Write down two strategies to challenge your assumptions, such as asking questions or consulting impartial sources.

Role-Playing Drill:

- Partner with someone. One person presents an argument that aligns with the other's beliefs, while the other practices questioning its validity and seeking alternative perspectives.

Key Takeaway

The Confirmation Bias Bait manipulates trust by aligning with existing beliefs. Balance your comfort zone with a willingness to explore alternative views and verify information.

Chapter 77: The Anchoring Trap

When the First Number Sticks

You're shopping for a new sofa, and the salesperson shows you a high-end model priced at $4,000. It's beautiful but out of your budget. Then they show you another sofa for $2,000, emphasizing its "significant savings" compared to the first option. Relieved, you buy it, even though it's more expensive than you planned to spend.

This is the **Anchoring Trap**, where an initial value is presented to shape your perception of subsequent options. By anchoring your expectations to an exaggerated baseline, manipulators make alternatives seem more appealing, even when they're not ideal.

How It Works

1. **Establishing the Anchor:** Manipulators present an initial number, price, or value to create a reference point.
2. **Shaping Comparisons:** Future options are framed relative to the anchor, making them seem better or more reasonable.

3. **Fostering Quick Decisions:** Anchoring discourages deeper analysis, as people focus on the initial value rather than the broader context.

The Anchoring Trap works because humans are influenced by the first piece of information they encounter, even when it's irrelevant or exaggerated.

Real-Life Examples

1. **Retail Discounts:** Stores advertise inflated "original prices" to make standard discounts seem extraordinary.
2. **Salary Negotiations:** Employers start with a low offer, making slightly higher amounts seem generous, even if they're below market value.
3. **Luxury Comparisons:** Car dealerships show premium models first, making mid-range options seem affordable by comparison.

Why It Works

The Anchoring Trap thrives on three cognitive tendencies:

1. **Focus on Initial Values:** People instinctively reference the first number they encounter, even when irrelevant.
2. **Ease of Comparison:** Anchors simplify decisions by creating clear contrasts, even if they're misleading.
3. **Emotional Influence:** High anchors create relief when subsequent options feel like savings or compromises.

This tactic works because it shapes perceptions, steering decisions toward alternatives that may not truly align with your needs.

How to Spot the Anchoring Trap

1. **Ignore the Anchor:** Focus on whether the option meets your needs rather than comparing it to the initial value.
2. **Research Actual Costs:** Investigate average prices or values to establish an independent baseline.
3. **Evaluate Alternatives:** Consider options without referencing the anchor to assess their standalone value.

Exercise: Identify an Anchor

1. Think of a recent purchase influenced by an initial price or value. Reflect:
   - "Did I evaluate the option independently of the anchor?"
   - "Was the anchor relevant to my decision?"
2. Write down two ways to avoid anchoring in future decisions, such as comparing multiple sources or setting your own baseline.

Role-Playing Drill:

- Partner with someone. One person presents an anchored scenario, while the other practices identifying and ignoring the anchor to make an objective choice.

Key Takeaway

The Anchoring Trap steers decisions by presenting an initial value to shape perceptions. Focus on your own priorities and research independently to avoid being influenced by artificial benchmarks.

Chapter 78: The Illusory Truth Effect

When Illusion Becomes Belief

You hear a friend mention a popular diet plan claiming, **"You can lose 10 pounds in a week!"** Later, you see the same message in social media ads and hear it on a podcast. You decide to try the diet, only to find it unsustainable and potentially harmful.

This is the **Illusory Truth Effect**, where statements that are broadcasted on several platforms begin to feel accurate. Manipulators exploit this, building trust and confidence in false or misleading claims.

How It Works

1. **Message Frequency Reinforces Familiarity:** The more often a statement is heard or seen, the more familiar it feels, leading to perceived accuracy.

2. **Reducing Effortful Thinking:** Familiar statements are processed more easily by the brain, creating a shortcut to perceived truth.
3. **Widespread Messaging:** Manipulators amplify their claims across multiple platforms to ensure consistent exposure.

The Illusory Truth Effect works because humans equate familiarity with reliability, making some falsehoods feel convincing over time.

Real-Life Examples

1. **Health Myths:** Claims such as **"Detox teas cleanse your system"** are repeated in ads, despite lacking scientific support.
2. **Political Narratives:** Politicians repeat misleading statistics or slogans to shape public opinion.
3. **Product Superiority Claims:** Brands repeatedly declare themselves as **"#1 in customer satisfaction"** without providing evidence.

Why It Works

This manipulation thrives on three psychological tendencies:

1. **Ease of Processing:** Familiar statements are easier to process, making them feel true.
2. **Trust in The Illusion:** Consistent exposure lowers resistance to the message, especially if it's unchallenged.
3. **Social Validation:** Hearing the same message from multiple sources creates the fake assurance of consensus.

This tactic works because it removes doubt by serving the same messaging frequently to individuals.

How to Spot the Illusory Truth Effect

1. **Seek Evidence:** Look for independent verification of repeated claims.
2. **Question the Source:** Identify whether the message originates from credible, unbiased sources.
3. **Recognize Patterns:** Watch out for messages that lack substance.

Exercise: Analyze Illusory Claims

1. Identify a belief or statement you've encountered multiple times. Reflect:
   - "Is this claim supported by evidence?"
   - "Where have I seen or heard it before?"
2. Write down two ways to verify information, such as consulting expert opinions or checking reliable sources.

Role-Playing Drill:

- Partner with someone. One person repeats a false claim, while the other practices identifying repetition and questioning its validity.

Key Takeaway

The Illusory Truth Effect aims to transform falsehoods into perceived truths. Always verify claims and avoid assuming accuracy based on familiarity alone.

Chapter 79: The Sunk Cost Fallacy Lever

This course isn't helping me, but I paid for it—so I have to finish.
But if it's not useful anymore, why keep going?

When Past Investments Cloud Judgment

You've subscribed to an online course but find it unhelpful after the first few weeks. Despite this, you continue attending, thinking, **"I've already paid for it, so I need to finish."** The time and money you've spent keep you committed, even though the course isn't benefiting you.

This is the **Sunk Cost Fallacy Lever**, where manipulators exploit your reluctance to abandon past investments, prompting continued commitment to bad decisions.

How It Works

1. **Highlighting Past Investments:** Manipulators remind you of the time, money, or effort you've already spent to keep you engaged.
2. **Triggering Emotional Attachments:** They use guilt or pride to tie your identity to the decision, making withdrawal feel like failure.

3. **Downplaying Future Costs:** The emphasis stays on what's been invested, diverting attention from the ongoing toll.

The Sunk Cost Fallacy Lever works because humans dislike the feeling of waste and prefer to justify previous decisions, even at a continued cost.

Real-Life Examples

1. **Subscription Renewals:** Services highlight your years of membership to encourage renewals, even if you no longer find value.
2. **Expensive Repairs:** Mechanics emphasize previous repair costs to justify further investment in a failing vehicle.
3. **Event Attendance:** People attend an event they don't enjoy simply because they paid for the tickets.

Why It Works

This manipulation leverages three cognitive tendencies:

1. **Aversion to Waste:** People feel compelled to "make the most" of past investments.
2. **Emotional Commitment:** Time and effort create a sense of personal attachment, discouraging change.
3. **Rationalization of Effort:** Victims justify poor decisions by focusing on what they've already given, rather than what they stand to lose.

This tactic works because it keeps people locked into cycles of diminishing returns.

How to Spot the Sunk Cost Fallacy Lever

1. **Focus on the Future:** Ask yourself, "What will continuing cost me, and is it worth it?"
2. **Separate Emotions from Logic:** Recognize when guilt or pride is influencing your decision.
3. **Evaluate Alternatives:** Consider whether walking away could open better opportunities.

Exercise: Reassess a Past Investment

1. Think of a recent situation where you felt stuck because of past investments. Reflect:
   - "Did continuing truly benefit me?"
   - "What alternatives could I have explored?"
2. Write down two steps to prioritize future value over past costs, such as setting clear limits on additional investments.

Role-Playing Drill:

- Partner with someone. One person highlights sunk costs, while the other practices focusing on future benefits and rational decision-making.

Key Takeaway

The Sunk Cost Fallacy Lever keeps people committed to poor decisions by emphasizing past investments. Shift your focus to future outcomes and recognize when it's better to let go.

Chapter 80: The Framing Effect Twist

When Presentation Changes Perception

You're shopping for health insurance and see two plans. One is described as covering **"90% of medical expenses,"** while the other highlights that **"you'll pay only 10% out-of-pocket."** Both plans offer the same coverage, but the first feels more generous, so you choose it without comparing the details further.

This is the **Framing Effect Twist**, where manipulators shape how you perceive choices by altering the way information is presented. By emphasizing positives or reframing negatives, they nudge you toward decisions that serve their interests, even when the underlying facts remain unchanged.

How It Works

1. **Highlighting the Positive Frame:** Manipulators emphasize benefits or favorable aspects of an option to make it seem more appealing.

2. **Minimizing the Negative Frame:** They present drawbacks in a way that makes them feel insignificant or even acceptable.
3. **Redirecting Focus:** By controlling the language or structure of information, manipulators guide your attention to what they want you to see.

The Framing Effect Twist works because humans rely on context to interpret information, often reacting emotionally to the way it's presented rather than evaluating the facts.

Real-Life Examples

1. **Hotel Rates:** A hotel advertises "Stay for just $150 per night" instead of the total cost of a week-long stay, making the expense seem less intimidating.
2. **Warranty Offers:** Electronics retailers promote "Peace of mind for just 50 cents a day" rather than stating the full yearly cost of the warranty.
3. **Insurance Plans:** Health insurers highlight "90% of claims paid on time" instead of mentioning that 10% are delayed, framing their service as reliable.

Why It Works

This tactic thrives on three psychological tendencies:

1. **Emotional Reactions to Words:** Positive language evokes trust or excitement, while negatives provoke caution.
2. **Simplified Decision-Making:** Framing reduces the need for deeper analysis, making quick choices more likely.
3. **Context-Driven Judgment:** People interpret information based on how it's framed, not its actual content.

The Framing Effect Twist works because it capitalizes on human reliance on context, nudging decisions toward what feels more appealing.

How to Spot the Framing Effect Twist

1. **Rephrase the Information:** Rewrite statements in different ways to see if the underlying meaning changes.

2. **Compare Options Objectively:** Focus on the actual data or facts, rather than the language used to describe them.
3. **Recognize Emotional Triggers:** Be wary of words or phrases designed to elicit strong feelings.

Exercise: Reframe a Decision

1. Think of a recent decision influenced by how it was framed. Reflect:
    - "Would I feel differently if the wording were changed?"
    - "Did the framing emphasize benefits or minimize drawbacks?"
2. Write down two strategies to evaluate options based on facts, such as creating a pros-and-cons list.

Role-Playing Drill:

- Partner with someone. One person presents the same information with different framing (positive vs. negative), while the other practices identifying the true meaning behind the language.

Key Takeaway

The Framing Effect Twist manipulates decisions by shaping how information is presented. To counter this, focus on the underlying facts and avoid being swayed by emotional or persuasive language.

Section 5: Defensive Mastery

This final section equips you with the tools to defend against some of the most insidious and subtle manipulation tactics. Each chapter dissects a specific technique, revealing how manipulators operate and offering actionable strategies to protect yourself. Whether the attack comes through emotional appeals, digital deception, or psychological pressure, you'll learn to recognize the signs, respond with confidence, and stay in control.

Chapter 81: The Psychological Takeover

How Emotional Intensity Undermines Logic

You're negotiating a refund for a defective product, and the representative becomes increasingly agitated, raising their voice and flooding the conversation with emotional outbursts. Overwhelmed, you relent and accept store credit instead of insisting on a full refund.

This is the **Psychological Takeover**, where manipulators use intense emotions — such as anger, despair, or excitement — to hijack logical reasoning. By creating an emotionally charged environment, they overwhelm your ability to think clearly, pressuring you into compliance.

How It Works

1. **Escalating Emotions:** Manipulators amplify feelings of fear, anger, or urgency to create mental overwhelm.

2. **Diverting Focus:** Emotional intensity distracts you from evaluating the situation critically or questioning their intentions.
3. **Demanding Immediate Action:** Once logic is disrupted, manipulators push for decisions before emotions settle.

The Psychological Takeover works because humans prioritize emotional responses over rational thinking in high-stress situations.

Real-Life Examples

1. **Aggressive Sales Tactics:** High-pressure salespeople use excitement and urgency to rush buyers into expensive purchases.
2. **Personal Conflicts:** Manipulators in relationships escalate arguments to guilt or pressure their partners into giving in.
3. **Workplace Demands:** A manager raises their voice and emphasizes tight deadlines to pressure employees into taking on extra tasks without question.

Why It Works

This tactic exploits three key psychological tendencies:

1. **Emotional Overload:** High-intensity emotions block rational thought, creating a reactive mindset.
2. **Desire to De-escalate:** Targets comply to reduce emotional tension or avoid further conflict.
3. **Rushed Decisions:** Emotional urgency prompts snap judgments, leaving little time for reflection.

This tactic works because it capitalizes on heightened emotions to cloud judgment and force hasty actions.

How to Spot the Psychological Takeover

1. **Recognize Emotional Shifts:** Notice when a conversation becomes overly heated or dramatic.
2. **Pause and Reflect:** Take a step back to let emotions subside before responding.
3. **Ask for Time:** Request a break to assess the situation calmly and regain focus.

Exercise: Practice Emotional Detachment

1. Recall a situation where you felt pressured during an emotional conversation. Reflect:
   - "How could I have paused to regain control?"
   - "What questions could I have asked to slow things down?"
2. Write down two strategies to use when facing emotional pressure, such as taking deep breaths or stepping away momentarily.

Role-Playing Drill:

- Partner with someone. One person practices escalating emotions, while the other works on staying calm and responding logically.

Key Takeaway

The Psychological Takeover relies on emotional intensity to overpower logical reasoning. Stay calm, pause for reflection, and avoid rushing into decisions under emotional pressure.

Chapter 82: The False Helper

When Someone Has Hidden Motives

You're at a crowded train station, struggling to carry your luggage up the stairs. A stranger offers assistance, smiling and insisting they only want to help. While they carry your bag, you notice later that your wallet is missing.

This is the **False Helper**, where manipulators use the guise of goodwill to lower your defenses. By appearing generous and selfless, they gain trust and access, paving the way for exploitation.

How It Works

1. **Establishing Trust Through Kindness:** Manipulators perform helpful gestures to appear trustworthy and approachable.
2. **Identifying Vulnerabilities:** They target moments when victims are distracted, overwhelmed, or in need of assistance.

3. **Capitalizing on Gratitude:** By earning appreciation, manipulators create a sense of obligation or lower the target's suspicion.

The False Helper works because humans are conditioned to trust and appreciate acts of kindness, making them less likely to question the helper's motives.

Real-Life Examples

1. **Online Scams:** Fraudsters offer free advice or tech support, then request sensitive information or payment for unnecessary services.
2. **In-Person Theft:** Pickpockets distract their targets by offering to help with directions or heavy bags while stealing from them.
3. **Professional Settings:** Colleagues offer to "help" with a project to gain access to confidential documents or ideas they can claim as their own.

Why It Works

This manipulation thrives on three psychological tendencies:

1. **Reciprocity Instinct:** People feel compelled to trust and repay acts of kindness.
2. **Lowered Defenses:** Acts of goodwill create an emotional barrier against suspicion.
3. **Gratitude Blindness:** Targets focus on the apparent kindness, missing potential red flags.

This tactic works because it combines trust-building with strategic exploitation, taking advantage of moments when victims are most vulnerable.

How to Spot the False Helper

1. **Question the Motive:** Ask yourself, "Is this act of kindness necessary, or could it serve a hidden purpose?"
2. **Stay Vigilant in Vulnerable Moments:** Be cautious when receiving help in high-stress or crowded environments.
3. **Set Boundaries:** Politely decline assistance if something feels off, and observe how the person reacts.

Exercise: Recognize Genuine Help

1. Reflect on a situation where you received unexpected help. Ask yourself:
   - "Did the person's behavior seem overly insistent or calculated?"
   - "Were there any hidden consequences of accepting the help?"
2. Write down two strategies to evaluate goodwill, such as staying alert to motives or maintaining control over personal belongings.

Role-Playing Drill:

- Partner with someone. One person offers unsolicited help in a simulated scenario, while the other practices politely setting boundaries and identifying suspicious behavior.

Key Takeaway

The False Helper manipulates trust by disguising exploitation as kindness. Stay alert and evaluate acts of goodwill, especially in vulnerable moments, to protect yourself from hidden motives.

Chapter 83: The Deceptive Question

When Questions Are Anything but Innocent

You're chatting with someone new at a networking event. They ask, **"What's your role at the company?"** followed by **"Do you handle client accounts or payments?"** The questions feel friendly and engaging, so you answer openly. Days later, you realize they've used the information to pose as you in an email sent to your clients.

This is the **Deceptive Question**, where manipulators mask their motives with casual or polite inquiries to gather personal, financial, or sensitive information. By disguising their true intent, they lure targets into revealing more than they realize.

How It Works

1. **Building Rapport:** Manipulators establish a friendly or professional connection to create a sense of safety.

2. **Using Open-Ended Questions:** They ask broad or seemingly innocent questions to encourage detailed responses.
3. **Extracting Key Details:** They steer the conversation toward information that can be exploited, such as passwords, schedules, or sensitive access points.

The Deceptive Question works because humans are naturally inclined to answer questions in social or professional settings without suspicion, especially when rapport has been established.

Real-Life Examples

1. **Charity Fundraisers:** Individuals posing as charitable organizations ask questions about your income or spending habits under the guise of assessing how much you can donate.
2. **Event Invitations:** Someone asks about your availability, workplace location, or routine under the pretense of inviting you to an exclusive networking event.
3. **Neighborly Conversations:** A new neighbor casually inquires about your home's security features or the schedules of others in the community, masking intentions to gather exploitable details.

Why It Works

This tactic relies on three key psychological tendencies:

1. **Trust in Familiarity:** People are more likely to open up to someone who seems approachable or relatable.
2. **Desire to Be Polite:** Answering questions feels natural in social or professional interactions.
3. **Subtlety of Questions:** The manipulator's inquiries often feel harmless, lowering the target's guard.

The Deceptive Question works because it disguises exploitation as casual curiosity, encouraging targets to share sensitive details without realizing the risk.

How to Spot the Deceptive Question

1. **Evaluate the Context:** Ask yourself if the question is appropriate for the situation or if it feels out of place.

2. **Avoid Oversharing:** Stick to general answers and avoid giving unnecessary personal or sensitive details.
3. **Question the Questioner:** Politely inquire why they need specific information and observe their response.

Exercise: Filter Your Answers

1. Reflect on a recent conversation where someone asked personal questions. Ask yourself:
    - "Was the information I shared necessary?"
    - "Could they use any details I shared against me?"
2. Write down two strategies to limit your responses, such as giving broad answers or redirecting the conversation.

Role-Playing Drill:

- Partner with someone. One person asks open-ended questions, while the other practices identifying and avoiding over-disclosure.

Key Takeaway

The Deceptive Question uses subtle inquiries to extract critical information under the guise of casual conversation. Protect yourself by staying alert, questioning motives, and limiting the details you share.

Chapter 84: The "Too Good to Be True" Trap

How Temptation Overrides Caution

You receive an email that says, **"You've been selected for an all-expenses-paid vacation!"** Excited, you click the link and follow instructions to claim your prize. Only later do you realize the catch: you've shared your personal information, fallen for a scam, or been charged "processing fees" for a trip that doesn't exist.

This is the **"Too Good to Be True" Trap**, where manipulators exploit irresistible offers to lure people into making hasty decisions. These offers are designed to appeal to emotions like excitement or greed, distracting targets from asking critical questions.

How It Works

1. **Creating an Irresistible Offer:** Manipulators promise unbelievable rewards, such as huge discounts, free prizes, or exclusive opportunities.

2. **Building Urgency:** Victims are pressured to act quickly before the offer "expires," leaving no time to verify its authenticity.
3. **Masking Hidden Costs:** The full terms and consequences of the offer are obscured, ensuring that victims only realize the risks after they've taken the bait.

The "Too Good to Be True" Trap works because the promise of a reward overrides critical thinking, leading people to act recklessly.

Real-Life Examples

1. **Lottery Scams:** Emails claim you've won a foreign lottery but require an upfront fee to process your "winnings."
2. **Unbelievable Discounts:** Ads promise high-value items like smartphones or luxury handbags at impossibly low prices, leading to non-existent or counterfeit products.
3. **Job Offers:** Scammers offer "work-from-home" jobs with high pay but request upfront fees for training or equipment.

Why It Works

This manipulation thrives on three psychological tendencies:

1. **Excitement Over Caution:** The allure of a reward clouds judgment and reduces doubt.
2. **Desire for Exclusivity:** Offers make targets feel special, encouraging quick action.
3. **Trust in Appearances:** Professional-looking websites give a false sense of legitimacy.

This tactic works because it appeals to emotional desires while minimizing the opportunity for rational evaluation.

How to Spot the "Too Good to Be True" Trap

1. **Question the Offer:** Ask, "Is this offer realistic? Why would they give away such a large reward?"
2. **Research the Source:** Verify the sender or company offering the deal through independent channels.

3. **Look for Hidden Terms:** Check for vague conditions, hidden fees, or requests for personal or financial information.

Exercise: Evaluate Tempting Offers

1. Think of a time when you were tempted by an unbelievable deal or prize. Reflect:
   - "Did I verify the offer's authenticity?"
   - "What questions should I have asked before acting?"
2. Write down two steps to assess future offers, such as researching the source or comparing similar deals.

Role-Playing Drill:

- Partner with someone. One person presents an enticing but unrealistic offer, while the other practices identifying red flags and asking clarifying questions.

Key Takeaway

The "Too Good to Be True" Trap manipulates emotions with tempting offers. Always verify the details and question offers that seem overly generous or unrealistic.

Chapter 85: The False Urgency Alarm

When Pressure Overrides Caution

You're booking tickets for a concert, and a banner on the website says, **"Only 5 seats left!"** Feeling the rush, you complete the purchase without checking the seating arrangement or refund policy. Later, you find better seats on a different platform — still available at a lower price. The "limited seats" message wasn't true.

This is the **False Urgency Alarm**, a manipulation tactic that fabricates pressure to force quick decisions. By making opportunities seem fleeting, manipulators prevent targets from fully analyzing their options, increasing the chances of impulsive actions.

How It Works

1. **Simulating Restrictions:** Manipulators create fake limited stock or exclusive deadlines to make offers seem rare.

2. **Triggering Decision Fatigue:** The rush to act overwhelms logical thinking and encourages emotional responses.
3. **Hiding Flaws or Risks:** Urgency makes people overlook essential details, like hidden fees or poor quality.

The False Urgency Alarm works because humans instinctively prioritize immediate action when faced with perceived scarcity or pressure, often neglecting thorough evaluation.

Real-Life Examples

1. **Limited-Edition Drops:** Online stores claim items are part of an exclusive release, but restock the same products regularly.
2. **Travel Deals:** Airline websites display messages like **"Only 2 seats left at this price!"** even when more seats are available, creating unnecessary pressure to book quickly.
3. **Real Estate Listings:** Agents emphasize phrases like, **"This property won't stay on the market long!"** to prevent buyers from exploring alternatives.

Why It Works

This tactic preys on three psychological tendencies:

1. **Response to False Alarms:** People make faster, less considered decisions when they feel rushed.
2. **Focus on "Unique Offers":** Limited availability creates a sense of value and importance.
3. **Not Wanting to Miss Out:** The possibility losing out on a deal or opportunity amplifies urgency.

The False Urgency Alarm works because it creates artificial constraints that drive hasty decisions.

How to Spot the False Urgency Alarm

1. **Check for Consistency:** Look for evidence that the urgency is genuine, such as product availability across multiple platforms.
2. **Don't Act Immediately:** Take a moment to evaluate the offer, even if the deadline seems short.

3. **Investigate the Source:** Research the sender or company to confirm the legitimacy of their claims.

Exercise: Practice Pausing Under Pressure

1. Recall a recent situation where you felt rushed to act. Reflect:
    - "What would I have done differently with more time?"
    - "Was the urgency real or manufactured?"
2. Write down two strategies to create space for evaluation, such as setting a personal time limit before responding.

Role-Playing Drill:

- Partner with someone. One person creates an artificial sense of urgency, while the other practices pausing and asking clarifying questions before deciding.

Key Takeaway

The False Urgency Alarm pressures decisions by fabricating time constraints. Slow down, verify the claims, and ensure your actions align with your priorities.

Chapter 86: The Trust Shortcut

When Familiarity Opens the Door

You're on vacation in a foreign city when someone approaches you and says, **"Aren't you from Chicago? I used to live there!"** Excited by the connection, you chat freely, sharing details about your plans and hotel. Hours later, you realize your room was broken into—and you suspect the person used your shared details to target you.

This is the **Trust Shortcut**, where manipulators create instant familiarity to lower defenses. By mimicking social cues, finding common ground, or appearing knowledgeable, they establish trust without earning it, leaving their targets vulnerable to exploitation.

How It Works

1. **Creating a Connection:** Manipulators identify or invent similarities — such as shared hometowns, schools, or hobbies — to build a sense of rapport.

2. **Mimicking Behavior:** They mirror body language, tone, or speech patterns to make interactions feel comfortable and natural.
3. **Leveraging the Bond:** Once trust is established, they subtly introduce requests, extract information, or exploit the relationship.

The Trust Shortcut works because humans tend to trust those who seem similar or relatable, often overlooking inconsistencies.

Real-Life Examples

1. **Job Scams:** Fraudsters pose as former employees of a company, claiming insider knowledge to build trust during recruitment or investment schemes.
2. **Tourist Cons:** Manipulators pose as fellow travelers, sharing fabricated experiences to gain trust and steal belongings.
3. **Neighborhood Scams:** Fraudsters pose as new neighbors, mentioning nearby landmarks or community events to seem credible. They then exploit this trust to borrow money, gain access to homes, or gather sensitive information.

Why It Works

This manipulation tactic succeeds because of three key psychological tendencies:

1. **Bias Toward Similarity:** People trust those they perceive as being like themselves.
2. **Desire for Belonging:** Establishing common ground makes interactions feel meaningful and safe.
3. **Assumed Credibility:** Targets are less likely to question someone who seems relatable or familiar.

The Trust Shortcut works because it creates the illusion of authenticity, allowing manipulators to remove doubt.

How to Spot the Trust Shortcut

1. **Verify Claims of Familiarity:** Ask follow-up questions to confirm shared details or connections.

2. **Be Cautious of Over-Friendliness:** Stay alert if someone seems overly eager to bond or establish trust.
3. **Trust Your Instincts:** If something feels too convenient or "perfect," take a step back to reassess.

Exercise: Practice Verifying Connections

1. Recall a situation where someone quickly earned your trust by mentioning a shared connection. Reflect:
   - "Did I ask questions to confirm their story?"
   - "Could I have been more cautious?"
2. Write down two strategies for verifying shared connections, such as asking for specific details or consulting mutual acquaintances.

Role-Playing Drill:

- Partner with someone. One person pretends to establish a quick connection based on a shared interest or background, while the other practices asking follow-up questions to verify the claim.

Key Takeaway

The Trust Shortcut manipulates social cues and similarities to create false trust. Always verify claims of familiarity and be mindful of overly friendly interactions to avoid being exploited.

Chapter 87: The Credential Snatch

I just logged in after getting an email about a failed payment.
Did you check the URL? That might've been a fake page.

When Security Is an Illusion

You receive an email from what appears to be your streaming service: **"Your subscription payment failed. Log in now to avoid account suspension."** The email includes a link to a login page that looks identical to the official site. Without hesitation, you enter your username and password, only to discover later that your account was hacked, and someone made unauthorized purchases using your payment details.

This is the **Credential Snatch**, where manipulators replicate trusted systems or platforms to steal login information. By creating authentic-looking interfaces and presenting fabricated scenarios, they exploit trust and gain unauthorized access to sensitive accounts or personal data.

How It Works

1. **Imitating Legitimate Interfaces:** Manipulators replicate login pages, emails, or apps to collect credentials.
2. **Preying on Confidence:** They design their traps to look as authentic as possible, relying on visual and contextual familiarity.
3. **Creating a False Narrative:** Scammers fabricate stories like "suspicious activity" or "account upgrades" to compel action.

The Credential Snatch works because people trust familiar platforms and often act quickly in response to perceived threats.

Real-Life Examples

1. **Gaming Account Theft:** Fraudsters create fake promotions for in-game rewards, directing players to login pages that steal their gaming credentials.
2. **E-Learning Platform Hoaxes:** Students are tricked into logging into counterfeit online learning portals, compromising their account details and grades.
3. **Fake Charity Websites:** During donation drives, scammers replicate legitimate charity sites, urging users to log in and provide payment information.

Why It Works

This tactic succeeds because of three key factors:

1. **Visual Authenticity:** Replicating trusted interfaces lowers suspicion.
2. **Urgency to Act:** Fabricated threats encourage immediate responses.
3. **Blind Trust:** People assume familiar communication is legitimate and act without verifying.

How to Spot the Credential Snatch

1. **Carefully Review URLs:** Check for inconsistencies or slight alterations in web addresses.
2. **Avoid Clicking Links:** Navigate directly to official websites rather than using links in emails or texts.

3. **Confirm Requests:** Contact the organization directly to verify any urgent claims.

Exercise: Test Credential Awareness

1. Review a recent email or text asking for login details. Ask:
   - "Did I check the sender's authenticity?"
   - "Was the request urgent or unusual?"
2. Write down two steps to evaluate login pages, such as checking URLs or using official apps.

Role-Playing Drill:

- Partner with someone. One person creates a fake login scenario, while the other practices identifying red flags and verifying legitimacy.

Key Takeaway

The Credential Snatch manipulates trust to extract sensitive login details. Stay vigilant, verify sources, and avoid entering credentials without double-checking authenticity.

Chapter 88: The Power Pose

When Authority Is Faked

A man in a suit approaches you at a train station, flashing a badge and claiming to be from transportation services. He demands your ticket and ID for verification. You comply, only to later find out he wasn't an official employee — he was gathering personal data for identity theft.

This is the **Power Pose**, where manipulators adopt the appearance or behavior of authority figures to intimidate and coerce compliance. By leveraging symbols of authority, such as uniforms, badges, or professional language, they exploit the natural tendency to defer to those in power.

How It Works

1. **Mimicking Authority:** Manipulators dress, speak, or act in ways that align with trusted authority figures.
2. **Creating Pressure:** They use commanding tones or intimidating stances to discourage questioning.

3. **Demanding Compliance:** Targets are conditioned to follow authority, making them less likely to resist.

The Power Pose works because humans are taught to respect and obey perceived authority, even when the legitimacy is questionable.

Real-Life Examples

1. **Fake Inspectors:** Scammers pose as safety inspectors, demanding access to homes or businesses under false pretenses.
2. **Impostor Officials:** Fraudsters pretend to be law enforcement officers to extract personal information or payments.
3. **Corporate Impostors:** Manipulators pose as senior executives, pressuring employees to share confidential data.

Why It Works

This tactic relies on three psychological principles:

1. **Respect for Authority:** People are conditioned to trust those who appear to hold power.
2. **Fear of Repercussions:** The risk of disobeying authority discourages resistance.
3. **Lack of Verification:** Targets rarely question authority figures, assuming legitimacy.

How to Spot the Power Pose

1. **Ask for Verification:** Request credentials or contact the organization they claim to represent.
2. **Question the Context:** Assess whether the person's behavior aligns with their supposed authority.
3. **Trust Your Instincts:** If something feels off, take time to verify before complying.

Exercise: Practice Questioning Authority

1. Reflect on a situation where you complied with an authority figure. Ask yourself:
    - "Did I verify their legitimacy?"
    - "Was their request reasonable for the situation?"

2. Write down two steps to assess authority, such as checking credentials or consulting a second opinion.

Role-Playing Drill:

- Partner with someone. One person pretends to be an authority figure, while the other practices asking for verification and maintaining composure.

Key Takeaway

The Power Pose uses symbols of authority to manipulate and intimidate. Always verify claims of authority before complying, and don't hesitate to ask questions.

Chapter 89: The Unverified Crisis

When Fake Emergencies Create Chaos

You receive a phone call late at night. The voice on the other end says, **"Your cousin has been arrested while traveling abroad. We need $3,000 immediately to post bail."** Without verifying, you wire the money, only to discover later that your cousin was never in trouble, and the caller was a scammer.

This is the **Unverified Crisis**, where manipulators fabricate emergencies to evoke fear and urgency. The target's emotional response overrides logic, leading to ill-considered actions such as transferring money or sharing sensitive information.

How It Works

1. **Choosing a Vulnerable Target:** Scammers target individuals who are likely to respond emotionally, such as family members or business owners.
2. **Crafting a Plausible Crisis:** They create situations that feel urgent and realistic, like accidents, legal trouble, or compromised accounts.

3. **Demanding Immediate Action:** Victims are pressured to act quickly, giving them little time to question or verify the situation.

The Unverified Crisis works because fear and urgency cloud rational thinking, making people act without considering alternatives.

Real-Life Examples

1. **Grandparent Scams:** Fraudsters pretend to be a grandchild in trouble, asking for money to handle an emergency.
2. **Disaster Relief Hoaxes:** Criminals pretend to represent aid organizations, claiming a family member has been affected by a natural disaster and urgently needs financial assistance.
3. **Ransom Scams:** Targets are told a loved one has been kidnapped, with demands for immediate payment to ensure their safety.

Why It Works

This manipulation succeeds due to three psychological factors:

1. **Emotional Overload:** Fear and concern for loved ones overshadow logic and reduce doubt.
2. **Authority in Crisis:** The caller often claims to be a figure of authority (a police officer or doctor), adding credibility.
3. **Time Pressure:** The urgency of the crisis discourages verification, forcing thoughtless decisions.

How to Spot the Unverified Crisis

1. **Pause and Assess:** Ask yourself if the situation makes sense before taking action.
2. **Verify the Claim:** Contact the supposed authority figure or individual involved using official channels.
3. **Be Wary of Payments:** Avoid sending money or sharing information until the situation is confirmed.

Exercise: Prepare for Crisis Scenarios

1. Think of a time you felt rushed to act in an emergency. Reflect:
   - "What steps did I take to verify the situation?"
   - "How could I have handled it better?"
2. Write down two strategies to verify emergencies, such as contacting the person directly or consulting a trusted source.

Role-Playing Drill:

- Partner with someone. One person creates a fake crisis scenario, while the other practices asking questions and verifying details before acting.

Key Takeaway

The Unverified Crisis manipulates emotions by fabricating emergencies. Stay calm, verify claims, and never act impulsively in high-pressure situations.

Chapter 90: The Oversharing Setup

When Friendly Chats Turn Dangerous

You're sitting at a café when a stranger strikes up a conversation. They ask, **"Do you work nearby? What's your favorite thing about your office?"** Flattered by their interest, you share details about your job and schedule. Later, you realize your office experienced a break-in, and the stranger may have used your answers to plan it.

This is the **Oversharing Setup**, where manipulators use casual conversation to subtly extract useful information. By appearing friendly and non-threatening, they trick targets into divulging sensitive details.

How It Works

1. **Starting Small:** Manipulators begin with harmless questions to establish rapport.

2. **Earning Trust:** They act interested and supportive, encouraging the target to open up.
3. **Extracting Key Details:** They steer the conversation toward information that can be exploited, like routines, job details, or personal preferences.

The Oversharing Setup works because people are naturally inclined to talk about themselves, especially when prompted by a seemingly friendly person.

Real-Life Examples

1. **Workplace Espionage:** A competitor poses as a friendly stranger, asking employees about company operations or upcoming projects.
2. **Burglar Planning:** Manipulators ask about vacation plans or daily schedules to identify when a home will be empty.
3. **Networking Event Manipulation:** Scammers attend professional networking events, posing as industry insiders. They ask detailed questions about business strategies or personal finances, later using the information for fraudulent schemes.

Why It Works

This tactic thrives on three psychological tendencies:

1. **Desire to Connect:** People enjoy talking about themselves and sharing experiences.
2. **Lowered Defenses:** Casual conversation feels safe, making targets less cautious.
3. **Unaware Risks:** Most people don't realize how seemingly minor details can be exploited.

How to Spot the Oversharing Setup

1. **Watch Out For Probing Questions:** Notice if the other person consistently steers the conversation toward personal details.
2. **Limit Information:** Share only general answers, especially with strangers or new acquaintances.
3. **Redirect the Conversation:** Politely shift topics if the questions feel too specific or invasive.

Exercise: Practice Limiting Information

1. Think of a recent casual conversation where you shared personal details. Reflect:
   - "Did I reveal more than necessary?"
   - "Could this information be used against me?"
2. Write down two strategies to manage oversharing, such as keeping answers vague or steering conversations to neutral topics.

Role-Playing Drill:

- Partner with someone. One person asks friendly but probing questions, while the other practices identifying and limiting oversharing.

Key Takeaway

The Oversharing Setup uses casual conversation to extract sensitive details. Stay mindful of what you share, especially with people you don't know well.

Chapter 91: The False Confirmation Request

When Confirming Leads to Compromising

You receive a text that says, **"Your bank account has been temporarily locked. Reply with your account PIN to unlock it."** Concerned about accessing your funds, you respond immediately. Moments later, you notice unauthorized transactions in your account.

This is the **False Confirmation Request**, where manipulators send fake prompts to trick people into sharing sensitive details. By appearing legitimate and urgent, these requests exploit the target's instinct to resolve issues quickly.

How It Works

1. **Mimicking Official Communication:** Scammers craft messages that look like they're from trusted organizations.

2. **Creating a Sense of Necessity:** Victims are prompted to act immediately to avoid consequences such as account suspension.
3. **Extracting Information:** Once the target provides the requested details, scammers use them for unauthorized access.

The False Confirmation Request works because people often prioritize solving problems over verifying authenticity.

Real-Life Examples

1. **Fake Password Resets:** Emails ask users to "confirm" their passwords, leading to compromised accounts.
2. **Banking Scams:** Fraudsters pose as bank representatives, requesting account or card details to resolve non-existent issues.
3. **Job Application Scams:** Fraudsters send emails claiming to be recruiters, asking applicants to confirm personal information such as Social Security numbers or banking details to "finalize" a job offer.

Why It Works

This tactic thrives on three key factors:

1. **Trust in Familiarity:** Messages mimic real companies or services.
2. **Desire for Resolution:** People act quickly to avoid perceived problems or interruptions.
3. **Lack of Verification:** The sense of urgency overrides careful scrutiny.

How to Spot the False Confirmation Request

1. **Avoid Sharing Sensitive Details:** Legitimate companies rarely ask for passwords or account numbers via email or text.
2. **Verify the Source:** Contact the organization directly using official contact information.
3. **Look for Red Flags:** Check for generic greetings, spelling errors, or unusual requests.

Exercise: Recognize Legitimate Requests

1. Review recent emails or texts asking for account confirmations. Ask:
    - "Did the request seem unusual or urgent?"
    - "Was it from a verified source?"
2. Write down two steps to confirm legitimacy, such as contacting the company directly or reviewing account activity.

Role-Playing Drill:

- Partner with someone. One person creates a false confirmation scenario, while the other practices identifying and verifying legitimate requests.

Key Takeaway

The False Confirmation Request uses fake prompts to extract sensitive details. Always verify requests independently and avoid acting spur-of-the-moment to protect your information.

Chapter 92: The Hidden Link Trick

When Links Become Deceptive

You receive a text from a popular online retailer: **"Your recent order couldn't be processed. Click here to update your payment details."** The link appears to take you to the retailer's official site, complete with the same layout and branding. Trusting it, you enter your payment information. Hours later, you discover fraudulent charges on your credit card — the message was a scam.

This is the **Hidden Link Trick**, where attackers conceal harmful links under legitimate-looking text or buttons. By mimicking trusted platforms, they trick targets into unknowingly providing sensitive details, installing malware, or making unauthorized payments.

How It Works

1. **Crafting Convincing Messages:** Manipulators design messages that appear to come from trusted organizations, complete with logos and official wording.
2. **Hiding the URL:** The visible link text or button disguises the destination, making it look legitimate while redirecting to malicious sites.
3. **Prompting Urgent Action:** Messages often emphasize urgency, pressuring the recipient to act without checking the link.

The Hidden Link Trick works because it exploits the assumption that familiar-looking emails or texts are trustworthy, especially when the links appear authentic.

Real-Life Examples

1. **Package Delivery Scams:** Victims receive messages claiming, **“Your package couldn’t be delivered. Click here to reschedule,”** directing them to a fake website that collects payment details.
2. **Social Media Messages:** Fraudsters use hacked accounts to send messages like, **“Check out this video!”** with malicious links.
3. **Contest Winner Hoaxes:** Scammers send links claiming the recipient has won a prize. Clicking the link directs the target to a malicious site requesting personal or financial details to "claim" the prize.

Why It Works

This tactic thrives due to three psychological tendencies:

1. **Assumed Legitimacy:** Targets believe messages are from trusted sources.
2. **Overlooking the Details:** Many people don’t check URLs before clicking, especially on mobile devices.
3. **Emotional Triggers:** Urgency or sympathy distracts from verifying the link’s authenticity.

How to Spot the Hidden Link Trick

1. **Hover Over Links:** Check the URL that appears when hovering over a link to ensure it matches the expected destination.
2. **Inspect the Sender:** Verify the email address or phone number to confirm it matches the official source.
3. **Use Official Websites:** Instead of clicking links, manually navigate to the organization's website.

Exercise: Test Your Link Awareness

1. Review recent emails with links. Reflect:
   - "Did I check the URLs before clicking?"
   - "Did the link's destination match its appearance?"
2. Write down two strategies to verify links, such as hovering over the URL or avoiding clicking links in unsolicited messages.

Role-Playing Drill:

- Partner with someone. One person creates a fake email with a disguised link, while the other practices identifying and verifying the destination before clicking.

Key Takeaway

The Hidden Link Trick masks malicious URLs to steal information or install malware. Always check links before clicking, and rely on official sources for sensitive tasks.

Chapter 93: The Overload Maneuver

When Complexity Becomes a Weapon

You receive a phone call from someone claiming to be tech support. They instruct you to open your computer settings and begin describing complicated technical steps.

Overwhelmed, you feel compelled to follow their instructions, even when they ask you to download a file you don't recognize. After the call, your computer is infected with malware, and the "support agent" vanishes.

This is the **Overload Maneuver**, where manipulators intentionally create a flood of information to confuse and distract their targets. By overwhelming victims, they make it harder to analyze the situation or recognize malicious intentions.

How It Works

1. **Generating Confusion:** Manipulators provide excessive or contradictory information to overwhelm the target.
2. **Creating a Sense of Expertise:** They appear knowledgeable, making victims feel pressured to comply.
3. **Distracting from Red Flags:** The complexity prevents targets from noticing inconsistencies or potential risks.

The Overload Maneuver works because people often defer to authority figures or "experts" when faced with confusing situations.

Real-Life Examples

1. **Tech Support Scams:** Fraudsters pose as IT experts, bombarding victims with technical jargon to trick them into installing malware.
2. **Fake Healthcare Hoaxes:** Scammers provide lengthy, detailed explanations of fake medical treatments or insurance policies, confusing victims into purchasing fraudulent services or sharing sensitive information.
3. **Online Terms and Conditions:** Some malicious apps or websites bury harmful clauses in lengthy terms to confuse users into agreeing.

Why It Works

This tactic succeeds due to three psychological factors:

1. **Cognitive Overload:** Too much information reduces the ability to think critically.
2. **Reliance on Authority:** Targets assume the manipulator's expertise is genuine.
3. **Urgency to Comply:** The overwhelming nature of the situation pushes people to act quickly.

How to Spot the Overload Maneuver

1. **Pause and Simplify:** Take a moment to break down the information and assess it step by step.
2. **Verify Claims:** Cross-check any advice or instructions with a trusted source before acting.

3. **Trust Your Instincts:** If something feels unnecessarily complex, it may be intentional.

Exercise: Manage Overload Scenarios

1. Recall a time when you felt overwhelmed by excessive information. Reflect:
   - "How did I react to the situation?"
   - "Could I have taken steps to simplify it?"
2. Write down two strategies for managing overload, such as asking for clarification or consulting a second opinion.

Role-Playing Drill:

- Partner with someone. One person plays a manipulator flooding the other with information, while the second practices identifying key points and resisting pressure to act.

Key Takeaway

The Overload Maneuver uses excessive information to confuse and distract. Slow down, simplify the situation, and check claims before taking action.

Chapter 94: The Emotional Leverage

When Emotions Become Tools of Manipulation

Imagine you get a frantic call from someone claiming to be a relative: **"I got arrested, and I need you to send money immediately for bail!"** The voice sounds convincing, and the panic in their tone feels real. Distraught, you wire the money without asking questions. Later, you realize it wasn't your loved one — it was a scammer exploiting your emotions to steal from you.

This is **Emotional Leverage**, where manipulators weaponize trust, guilt, fear, or love to cloud judgment. By targeting deep-seated feelings, they bypass critical thinking, making it easier to gain compliance.

How It Works

1. **Establishing Trust:** The manipulator pretends to be someone you know or a trusted figure, like a friend or family member.

2. **Triggering an Emotional Reaction:** They use scenarios that evoke strong emotions, such as fear, guilt, or urgency.
3. **Exploiting Vulnerability:** Once you're emotionally invested, they push for immediate action, like transferring money or sharing sensitive information.

Emotional Leverage works because feelings like love, guilt, and fear often override logic, especially in high-pressure situations.

Real-Life Examples

1. **Adoption Fraud:** Manipulators claim to be raising funds for a child's adoption, sharing emotional stories and fabricated photos to solicit donations.
2. **Fake Medical Fundraisers:** Fraudsters create campaigns for non-existent surgeries or treatments, exploiting people's compassion to raise money.
3. **Animal Rescue Cons:** Scammers post heart-wrenching stories of abused animals needing urgent care, asking for financial support to cover "veterinary costs."

Why It Works

This tactic thrives on three key psychological factors:

1. **Emotional Intensity:** Strong feelings cloud judgment, making targets more susceptible.
2. **Urgency of Connection:** Personal bonds or the appearance of trust encourage swift action.
3. **Fear of Consequences:** The perceived cost of inaction (e.g., harm to a loved one) overrides caution.

How to Spot Emotional Leverage

1. **Verify the Situation:** Contact the person or organization directly using official channels.
2. **Pause and Reflect:** Take time to process the emotions before acting.
3. **Look for Manipulative Patterns:** Be wary of messages that evoke panic or guilt to compel action.

Exercise: Reflect on Emotional Decisions

1. Think of a time when an emotional appeal influenced a decision. Reflect:
   - "What emotions drove my choice?"
   - "Would I have acted differently with more time?"
2. Write down two strategies to manage emotional situations, like verifying claims or seeking a second opinion.

Role-Playing Drill:

- Partner with someone. One person pretends to be a manipulator using emotional appeals, while the other practices staying calm and verifying the situation.

Key Takeaway

Emotional Leverage preys on strong feelings to manipulate decisions. Pause, verify, and think critically to protect yourself from these tactics.

Chapter 95: The Insider Ploy

Hey, I'm from the downtown branch. Can you buzz me into the server room?
Let me check with the manager first.
STAFF

When Familiarity Breeds Deception

A person walks into your workplace wearing a uniform and holding a clipboard. They greet you warmly, saying, **"I'm here to check the office equipment for updates. Can you let me into the server room?"** Believing they're an employee from another branch, you grant access. Hours later, IT discovers a data breach — this person wasn't from your company at all.

This is the **Insider Ploy**, where manipulators pose as trusted insiders to exploit systems or gain access to sensitive information. By appearing familiar, they lower defenses and create opportunities to carry out their schemes.

How It Works

1. **Establishing Familiarity:** The manipulator pretends to be part of a group the target trusts, like co-workers or community members.
2. **Blending In:** They use uniforms, jargon, or insider knowledge to appear legitimate.

3. **Requesting Access:** Once trust is established, they ask for favors, access, or information that aids their agenda.

The Insider Ploy works because people naturally trust those they perceive as part of their in-group or organization.

Real-Life Examples

1. **Workplace Impersonation:** A fraudster claims to be an IT technician and asks employees for passwords to "fix" issues.
2. **Community Scams:** Someone poses as a neighbor or local service provider to gain entry to homes.
3. **Event Infiltration:** Scammers pretend to be event staff to steal personal belongings or gather information.

Why It Works

This tactic thrives on three psychological factors:

1. **Trust in Familiarity:** Targets are less likely to question someone who seems to belong.
2. **Deference to Authority:** Uniforms or professional language create a sense of legitimacy.
3. **Desire to Help:** People naturally want to assist those who appear to be part of their group.

How to Spot the Insider Ploy

1. **Verify Credentials:** Ask for identification or confirm their story with a trusted source.
2. **Be Cautious with Access:** Avoid granting entry or sharing information without proper verification.
3. **Look for Inconsistencies:** Watch for behavior or knowledge that doesn't align with their claimed role.

Exercise: Practice Verifying Insiders

1. Reflect on a time when someone claimed to be an insider. Ask:
   - "Did I confirm their credentials?"
   - "What steps could I have taken to verify their identity?"
2. Write down two strategies to verify insiders, such as requesting official IDs or consulting a manager.

Role-Playing Drill:

- Partner with someone. One person acts as an insider requesting access, while the other practices asking questions and verifying credentials.

Key Takeaway

The Insider Ploy leverages familiarity to gain trust and access. Always check identities, even when someone appears to belong.

Chapter 96: The Phony Transaction

When Payments Go to Scammers

You receive a text message claiming to be from your utility provider: **"Your electricity bill is overdue. Click here to avoid disconnection."** The link takes you to a page that looks just like the provider's payment portal. Panicking at the thought of losing power, you quickly enter your payment information and submit it. Hours later, you realize the payment never went to your utility company — it was a scammer's account.

This is the **Phony Transaction**, where fraudsters create fake payment requests to trick individuals into handing over money or sensitive financial information. By mimicking trusted sources and creating a sense of urgency, they exploit trust and fear to succeed.

How It Works

1. **Researching Targets:** Scammers identify individuals or businesses likely to receive similar invoices.
2. **Creating Plausible Requests:** They design invoices or emails that look official and legitimate.
3. **Demanding Urgency:** Messages often emphasize overdue payments or immediate action to pressure compliance.

The Phony Transaction works because people often process payments quickly, especially in busy environments.

Real-Life Examples

1. **Vendor Fraud:** Fraudsters send fake invoices to businesses, claiming to represent a legitimate supplier.
2. **Subscription Payment Scams:** Fake notices trick individuals into "paying" for service payments that apparently didn't go through.
3. **Fake Tax Payments:** Scammers pose as tax agencies, sending false notices about unpaid taxes.

Why It Works

This tactic thrives due to three psychological tendencies:

1. **Trust in Professional Design:** Fake invoices mimic legitimate formats.
2. **Fear of Consequences:** Targets worry about penalties for non-payment.
3. **Lack of Verification:** Busy environments reduce time to check requests.

How to Spot the Phony Transaction

1. **Check the Source:** Confirm the sender's identity before processing payments.
2. **Review Invoice Details:** Look for inconsistencies, like unusual account numbers or vague descriptions.
3. **Contact the Vendor:** Call or email the organization directly using official contact information.

Exercise: Audit Recent Invoices

1. Review your last five payment requests. Ask:
   - "Did I verify the source before processing the payment?"
   - "Were there any red flags I overlooked?"
2. Write down two steps to verify future invoices, such as cross-checking with known vendor records.

Role-Playing Drill:

- Partner with someone. One person creates a fake invoice scenario, while the other practices identifying red flags and checking the authenticity of the request.

Key Takeaway

The Phony Transaction exploits the trust and speed of payment processing. Always cross-check invoices and payment requests to prevent financial loss.

Chapter 97: The Digital Impersonator

When Identities Are Borrowed for Deception

You receive a message on a social media platform from someone claiming to be an old friend: **"Hey! It's been ages. I need a small favor—can you send me your phone number and email so we can reconnect?"** The request seems innocent, so you comply. Later, you discover the account was hacked, and your information is being used in other scams.

This is the **Digital Impersonator**, where scammers pose as trusted individuals or institutions online to extract personal or financial information. By assuming the identity of someone the victim knows or respects, they bypass doubt and gain compliance.

How It Works

1. **Creating Credibility:** Impersonators hack existing accounts or create fake profiles to appear authentic.
2. **Establishing Urgency:** They craft messages that encourage quick responses, such as needing help or resolving urgent issues.
3. **Extracting Information:** Once trust is gained, they request personal details, financial information, or even payments.

The Digital Impersonator works because it preys on the inherent trust people place in familiar identities and platforms.

Real-Life Examples

1. **Hacked Social Media Accounts:** Scammers use compromised profiles to send messages asking for money or personal information.
2. **Email Spoofing:** Fraudsters send emails from fake domains resembling legitimate companies, requesting sensitive data.
3. **Fake Customer Service Accounts:** Impersonators create accounts on social platforms, offering "help" to users and stealing their information.

Why It Works

This tactic thrives due to three psychological factors:

1. **Trust in Familiarity:** Victims are less likely to question requests from people or institutions they know.
2. **Speed Over Scrutiny:** Urgent requests prevent thorough checks.
3. **Emotional Connections:** Impersonators exploit personal bonds to compel action.

How to Spot the Digital Impersonator

1. **Verify Requests:** Contact the person or organization directly using official channels.
2. **Check for Inconsistencies:** Look for unusual grammar, tone, or behavior in messages.

3. **Be Cautious With Links:** Avoid clicking links from unexpected messages without confirming their authenticity.

Exercise: Analyze Recent Messages

1. Review the last three unexpected messages you received.
   - Were they consistent with the sender's usual tone?
   - Did they include suspicious requests or links?
2. Write down steps you'll take to verify future communications, such as calling the sender directly.

Role-Playing Drill:

- Partner with someone. One person acts as a scammer impersonating someone you know, while the other practices identifying red flags.

Key Takeaway

The Digital Impersonator exploits trust in familiar identities to gain sensitive information. Always confirm details to protect yourself.

Chapter 98: The Recurring Roulette

When Persistence Becomes Manipulation

You receive frequent texts from someone claiming to represent a charity. Each message starts friendly, like **"Hope you're doing well!"**, but over time, they become more insistent: **"Have you had a chance to donate yet? We're counting on you!"** Feeling guilty and worn down, you eventually send money—only to realize later the charity doesn't exist.

This is the **Recurring Roulette**, where manipulators use repeated attempts to wear down resistance, establish trust, or create guilt. By presenting themselves as consistent and reliable, they build a façade of credibility.

How It Works

1. **Establishing Presence:** The manipulator repeatedly contacts the target to stay on their radar.
2. **Building Trust:** Frequent interactions create the illusion of familiarity and credibility.
3. **Wearing Down Defenses:** Over time, the persistence erodes doubt and leads to compliance.

The Recurring Roulette works because repetition builds trust and makes targets feel obligated to respond.

Real-Life Examples

1. **Persistent Telemarketing Scams:** Fraudsters call repeatedly, using familiarity to gain trust and sell fraudulent products.
2. **Email Drip Scams:** Scammers send a series of emails with escalating urgency to pressure recipients into compliance.
3. **Subscription Fraud:** Fake services send recurring payment reminders, hoping the victim will pay without questioning.

Why It Works

This tactic thrives due to three psychological factors:

1. **Familiarity Through Repetition:** Frequent contact creates a false sense of trust.
2. **Emotional Fatigue:** Targets give in to stop the persistence.
3. **Perceived Obligation:** Consistent communication makes victims feel indebted to respond.

How to Spot the Recurring Roulette

1. **Set Boundaries:** Avoid responding to unsolicited messages or calls.
2. **Verify Identities:** Confirm the sender's legitimacy through official channels.
3. **Watch for Escalation:** Be cautious if messages become increasingly urgent or demanding.

Exercise: Identify Persistent Tactics

1. Reflect on a time you experienced persistent communication. Ask:
   - "Did their repeated attempts make me feel obligated?"
   - "What steps could I have taken to stop the manipulation?"
2. Write down two ways to handle repeated attempts, like blocking numbers or reporting spam.

Role-Playing Drill:

- Partner with someone. One person acts as a persistent scammer, while the other practices setting boundaries and ignoring pressure.

Key Takeaway

The Recurring Roulette relies on persistence to wear down resistance and build false trust. Stay firm, set boundaries, and double check all claims.

Chapter 99: The Open Door Trap

When Vulnerabilities Are Left Unchecked

You're at a coffee shop, and after finishing your drink, you head to the restroom, leaving your laptop unlocked. A passer-by takes advantage of the moment, quickly accessing your open emails to gather sensitive information. By the time you return, nothing seems amiss, but your data has been compromised.

This is the **Open Door Trap**, where manipulators exploit unsecured physical or digital spaces to access sensitive information or systems. A single lapse in vigilance is all they need to take advantage.

How It Works

1. **Identifying Vulnerabilities:** Scammers look for unattended devices or poorly secured accounts.
2. **Gaining Access:** They exploit physical proximity or unprotected networks to retrieve data.
3. **Executing Their Plan:** Once inside, they steal information or install malicious software.

The Open Door Trap works because even brief lapses in security create opportunities for exploitation.

Real-Life Examples

1. **Unattended Devices:** Laptops, phones, or tablets left unlocked in public spaces become targets for thieves.
2. **Public Wi-Fi Risks:** Unsecured connections allow attackers to intercept sensitive data.
3. **Open Accounts:** Forgotten logins on shared computers can be exploited for malicious purposes.

Why It Works

This tactic thrives on three psychological factors:

1. **Overconfidence in Safety:** Targets underestimate risks in familiar environments.
2. **Human Error:** Simple oversights, like forgetting to lock devices, create vulnerabilities.
3. **Speed of Exploitation:** Scammers act quickly to exploit brief moments of inattention.

How to Spot the Open Door Trap

1. **Secure Your Devices:** Always lock screens when stepping away.
2. **Avoid Public Wi-Fi:** Use a VPN or avoid transmitting sensitive data over unsecured networks.
3. **Log Out:** Ensure accounts are logged out when using shared devices.

Exercise: Secure Your Devices

1. List three physical or digital spaces where you often leave things unsecured.
   - Example: Laptops in public places, Wi-Fi networks, shared computers.
2. Write two steps to secure these spaces, like enabling auto-lock or using encrypted connections.

Role-Playing Drill:

- Practice identifying security vulnerabilities in a shared environment with a partner.

Key Takeaway

The Open Door Trap exploits unsecured spaces and devices. Vigilance and secure habits are key to avoiding these breaches.

Chapter 100: The Confidence Con

When Charm Masks Deception

You meet someone who introduces themselves as a successful entrepreneur. They speak with charisma, sharing tales of their past achievements and emphasizing their bold vision for the future. Excited by their energy and confidence, you agree to invest in their venture without conducting much research. Weeks later, you discover the entire project was a façade — they disappeared with your money.

This is the **Confidence Con**, where manipulators use charm, assertiveness, and persuasive storytelling to distract targets from potential risks. By projecting authority and certainty, they compel trust and compliance, often overriding logic.

How It Works

1. **Projecting Authority:** Manipulators use their demeanor, attire, and communication style to appear credible and trustworthy.
2. **Telling Convincing Stories:** They craft narratives designed to resonate emotionally, weaving in details that seem plausible.
3. **Suppressing Doubts:** Their boldness makes questioning them feel awkward or unnecessary, silencing doubt.

The Confidence Con succeeds because humans are naturally drawn to assertive individuals who seem to "know what they're doing."

Real-Life Examples

1. **Fraudulent Start-ups:** Scammers pitch fake investment opportunities with polished presentations and rehearsed pitches.
2. **Online Fibs:** Social media users exaggerate their credentials or success stories to promote dubious products or services, earning trust through their confident personas.
3. **Fake Experts:** Fraudsters pose as skilled professionals, confidently offering services they aren't qualified to perform.

Why It Works

This tactic thrives on three key psychological elements:

1. **Appeal to Authority:** People instinctively trust individuals who appear confident and self-assured.
2. **Emotional Connection:** Charm disarms defenses, making targets more likely to believe in the manipulator's intentions.
3. **Pressure to Trust:** Doubting someone so confident can feel socially uncomfortable, especially in public or professional settings.

How to Spot the Confidence Con

1. **Verify Claims:** Ask for tangible proof of credentials, achievements, or plans.
2. **Pause and Reflect:** Avoid being swept up in someone's enthusiasm; take time to evaluate.
3. **Trust Your Instincts:** If something feels off, don't ignore your gut. Confidence isn't proof of honesty.

Exercise: Challenge Bold Claims

1. Think of a time you were impressed by someone's confidence. Reflect on:
    - Did they provide evidence for their claims?
    - Were there any red flags you ignored?
2. Write down two questions you'll ask in the future when someone pitches an idea confidently.

Role-Playing Drill:

- Partner with someone to simulate a confident pitch. Practice asking critical questions to assess their claims.

Key Takeaway

The Confidence Con relies on charm and assertiveness to obscure doubts and risks. Stay grounded, ask questions, and always seek evidence.

Conclusion

You've now explored 100 human hacking strategies — manipulation tactics that range from exploiting emotions to leveraging cognitive biases and digital vulnerabilities. While the tactics may vary, their common goal is to influence decisions, often at the expense of logic, trust, or security. This knowledge is your armor, equipping you to recognize, resist, and neutralize manipulation in everyday situations.

Awareness Is Your First Line of Defense

Awareness is the cornerstone of protection. Whether it's spotting a suspicious email, questioning a too-good-to-be-true offer, or recognizing emotional triggers during negotiations, being vigilant allows you to pause and evaluate before acting. Manipulators rely on automatic, unthinking responses. By slowing down and applying critical thinking, you disrupt their strategy.

Practical Tip: Make it a habit to ask yourself, **"What's the motive behind this request?"** This single question can uncover hidden agendas.

Trust, But Verify

Trust is essential in human interactions, but blind trust can be a vulnerability. This book has highlighted countless examples where scammers exploited trust to achieve their goals. Moving forward, adopt a mindset of cautious curiosity—trusting others while verifying their claims. This balance ensures you remain open to genuine connections while protecting yourself from deceit.

Practical Tip: Always check the source of communication, whether it's an email, phone call, or social media message. If in doubt, contact the organization or person directly using official channels.

Embrace Critical Thinking

Manipulators thrive when emotions override logic. From false urgency to fabricated authority, they create scenarios that cloud judgment. Counter this by adopting a problem-solving mindset. Break down situations into facts, evaluate evidence, and assess potential outcomes.

Practical Tip: When faced with a high-pressure decision, take a moment to breathe and ask, **"What are the risks if I wait or say no?"** Most genuine opportunities will withstand scrutiny.

Practice Digital Hygiene

In today's interconnected world, many manipulation tactics are digital. Protecting yourself online is no longer optional—it's essential. Be wary of unsolicited links, create strong passwords, and avoid sharing personal information on unsecured platforms.

Practical Tip: Use tools such as two-factor authentication (2FA) and password managers to add layers of security to your accounts.

Resist Emotional Manipulation

Whether it's guilt, fear, or flattery, manipulators often target emotions to influence decisions. Recognizing these triggers is the key to neutralizing their power.

Practical Tip: When you feel an emotional reaction, pause and ask yourself, **"Is this emotion clouding my judgment?"** If so, take time to regain perspective before acting.

Build a Cautious Yet Open Mindset

This book has provided countless examples of how manipulators exploit assumptions. Going forward, question the surface and seek the deeper truth.

Practical Tip: Develop a mantra like, **"Is there more to this story?"** Use it whenever you encounter decisions that feel rushed or one-sided.

Share Your Knowledge

Knowledge is most powerful when shared. By teaching friends, family, and colleagues about the tactics you've learned, you create a ripple effect of awareness. Manipulators thrive in ignorance; your awareness can inspire others to protect themselves.

Practical Tip: Share examples of manipulation you've encountered and how you resisted. Real-life stories resonate and educate effectively.

A Final Word

The manipulation tactics outlined in this book are not just theoretical — they exist in daily life, from the workplace to online interactions. By mastering these insights, you've gained the power to recognize deception, protect your interests, and make confident decisions.

Remember: Awareness is your shield, critical thinking is your sword, and caution is your ally. Armed with these tools, you can navigate the complexities of human interaction with clarity and control. The world may be full of manipulative tactics, but you now have the strategies to stay one step ahead.

Appendix A: Your Quick Reference Guide

This appendix is your roadmap to navigating the strategies covered in this book. Each chapter is summarized in a single line, providing you with a quick refresher on the manipulation tactics and how to spot them. Use it as your go-to guide for recognizing, understanding, and countering manipulative behaviors in everyday life.

Section 1: Trust and Authority Exploits (Chapters 1–20)

Chapter 1: The Imposter Gambit

Pretend to be someone trustworthy to gain access or information.

Chapter 2: The Fake Badge

Exploit authority symbols like uniforms or titles to demand compliance.

Chapter 3: The Friendly Stranger

Build rapport to lower your defenses.

Chapter 4: The Expert Trap

Use technical language or complex jargon to confuse and intimidate.

Chapter 5: The Scarcity Hook

Claim resources are limited to create urgency and compel action.

Chapter 6: The Urgent Boss

Fake being a superior giving time-sensitive orders.

Chapter 7: The Insider Illusion

Pretend to be part of your team or company to build trust.

Chapter 8: The Overconfidence Play

Act so self-assured that others don't question your legitimacy.

Chapter 9: The Trust Triangle

Use a mutual connection or non-existing intermediary to gain trust.

Chapter 10: The Chain of Command

Exploit hierarchies by pressuring people to defer decisions to "superiors."

Chapter 11: The Name Drop

Mention known figures or organizations to establish credibility.

Chapter 12: The Call from the Top

Claim directives are coming from a higher authority to force compliance.

Chapter 13: The Financial Fraudster

Pose as a financial professional to steal money or access accounts.

Chapter 14: The Benevolent Guide

Pretend to help victims while secretly exploiting them.

Chapter 15: The Legal Threat

Use fake legal warnings to scare people into cooperation.

Chapter 16: The Medical Manipulator

Exploit trust in medical professionals to extract information or create panic.

Chapter 17: The Social Media Savior

Pose as a helpful social media contact to phish for details.

Chapter 18: The Customer Service Con

Mimic support agents to gain access to personal data or accounts.

Chapter 19: The Policeman's Bluff

Impersonate law enforcement to coerce or intimidate.

Chapter 20: The Religious Mask

Exploit faith or spiritual trust for manipulation.

Section 2: Emotional Manipulation Tactics (Chapters 21–40)

Chapter 21: The Fear Trigger

Incite fear to make people act without thinking.

Chapter 22: The Sympathy Card

Play on emotions of pity or compassion.

Chapter 23: The Guilt Lever

Exploit guilt to make someone comply.

Chapter 24: The Flattery Trap

Use excessive compliments to disarm scepticism.

Chapter 25: The Greed Ploy

Promise riches or rewards to lure people into a trap.

Chapter 26: The Pride Bull's Eye

Appeal to ego to make targets feel special or chosen.

Chapter 27: The Hope Hoax

Dangle false hope, like job offers.

Chapter 28: The Panic Button

Create a crisis to demand immediate action.

Chapter 29: The Shame Shove

Use shame to push compliance.

Chapter 30: The Empathy Bomb

Overload someone with emotional stories to cloud their judgment.

Chapter 31: The Anger Catalyst

Provoke anger to distract from logical thinking.

Chapter 32: The Nostalgia Smokescreen

Invoke fond memories to lower defenses.

Chapter 33: The Curiosity Click

Exploit curiosity to make someone click, open, or engage.

Chapter 34: The Imaginary Acquittance

Pretend to share interests to forge a connection.

Chapter 35: The Relationship Hijack

Use familial or romantic ties to manipulate trust.

Chapter 36: The Gratitude Debt

Offer a small favor to create a sense of obligation.

Chapter 37: The Exclusive Offer

Make someone feel special by offering "privileged" information or deals.

Chapter 38: The Ticking Timer

Create urgency with manufactured deadlines to force snap decisions.

Chapter 39: The Isolation Tactic

Separate targets from others to make them easier to manipulate.

Chapter 40: The Distraction Game

Overload someone's attention to sneak past defenses.

Section 3: Digital Manipulation and Online Scams (Chapters 41–60)

Chapter 41: The Clickbait Lure

Create irresistible headlines to drive action.

Chapter 42: The Baited Email

Send convincing emails designed to steal personal or financial information.

Chapter 43: The Digital Spy

Use social media to gather intelligence and exploit personal data.

Chapter 44: The Untrue Profile

Create personas to infiltrate social networks.

Chapter 45: The Malware Messenger

Send links that install malicious software.

Chapter 46: The Passcode Pilfer

Steal passwords, logins, and secure credentials through deception.

Chapter 47: The Catfisher

Pretend to be a romantic partner online to gain trust.

Chapter 48: The Deepfake Puppeteer

Use AI-generated content to impersonate real people.

Chapter 49: The Privacy Blackmail Trap

Blackmail someone using fabricated or stolen private data.

Chapter 50: The Ransomware Ruse

Encrypt someone's files and demand payment to unlock them.

Chapter 51: The Subscription Steal

Fake renewal notices that steal credit card details.

Chapter 52: The Survey Snare

Use fake polls to gather sensitive information.

Chapter 53: The Bogus Giveaway

Promise non-existing prizes in exchange for personal details.

Chapter 54: The Support Scam

Imitate tech support to gain remote control of devices.

Chapter 55: The Trojan Ad

Embed malicious code in seemingly harmless advertisements.

Chapter 56: The Public Wi-Fi Trap

Intercept data over insecure networks.

Chapter 57: The QR Code Con

Use fake QR codes to direct users to malicious sites.

Chapter 58: The Crypto Trap

Scam people through fraudulent cryptocurrency investments.

Chapter 59: The Influencer Lie

Pretend to be an influencer to promote scams.

Chapter 60: The Phone App Fraud

Create malicious apps disguised as useful tools.

Section 4: Exploiting Cognitive Biases (Chapters 61–80)

Chapter 61: The Authority Bias

Manipulate deference to perceived authority.

Chapter 62: The Recency Effect

Exploit recent events to sway decisions.

Chapter 63: The Commitment Trap

Secure a small agreement to trigger larger commitments.

Chapter 64: The Consensus Effect

Use fake popularity or testimonials to create trust.

Chapter 65: The Rarity Mirage

Make things appear more valuable by faking scarcity.

Chapter 66: The Extreme Evaluator

Present extreme comparisons to sway choices.

Chapter 67: The Availability Heuristic

Exploit what's top of mind to skew decisions.

Chapter 68: The Familiarity Bias

Use repetition to build misplaced trust.

Chapter 69: The Framing Effect

Manipulate perception by changing how information is presented.

Chapter 70: The Halo Effect

Exploit positive traits to create unwarranted trust.

Chapter 71: The Dunning-Kruger Effect Exploit

Convince people they know more than they actually do, prompting overconfidence.

Chapter 72: The Single Trait Trap

Use one positive characteristic to overshadow flaws or risks.

Chapter 73: The Loss Aversion Conundrum

Emphasize potential losses to pressure fast decision-making.

Chapter 74: The Status Quo Bias Manipulation

Exploit people's tendency to resist change, keeping them locked into a decision.

Chapter 75: The Optimism Bias Trick

Exploit the belief that "it won't happen to me" to lower caution.

Chapter 76: The Confirmation Bias Bait

Present information that aligns with existing beliefs to gain trust.

Chapter 77: The Anchoring Trap

Present an initial (often extreme) value to influence future decisions.

Chapter 78: The Illusory Truth Effect

Repeat falsehoods often enough that they feel true.

Chapter 79: The Sunk Cost Fallacy Lever

Keep people invested by reminding them how much they've already "spent" (time, money, effort).

Chapter 80: The Framing Effect Twist

Shape how choices are perceived by altering how they're presented.

Section 5: Defensive Mastery (Chapters 81–100)

Chapter 81: The Psychological Takeover

Manipulators create emotional intensity to override logical thinking.

Chapter 82: The False Helper

Disguise manipulation as acts of kindness or goodwill.

Chapter 83: The Deceptive Question

Seemingly innocent questions are designed to extract key information.

Chapter 84: The "Too Good to Be True" Trap

Attractive offers lure people into lowering their guard.

Chapter 85: The False Urgency Alarm

Creating a false sense of urgency pressures people into hasty decisions.

Chapter 86: The Trust Shortcut

Exploit recognizable details or patterns to quickly gain false trust.

Chapter 87: The Credential Snatch

Directly or indirectly manipulating people to reveal their login credentials.

Chapter 88: The Power Pose

Pretend to be an authority figure to intimidate or persuade.

Chapter 89: The Unverified Crisis

Inventing emergencies to force quick, unquestioned actions.

Chapter 90: The Oversharing Setup

Engaging people in conversation to casually extract sensitive information.

Chapter 91: The False Confirmation Request

Sending false prompts to confirm sensitive details like passwords or bank accounts.

Chapter 92: The Hidden Link Trick

Masking malicious links with legitimate-looking text or buttons.

Chapter 93: The Overload Maneuver

Flooding a target with complex or excessive information to confuse and distract.

Chapter 94: The Emotional Leverage

Exploit personal bonds and feelings to influence decisions.

Chapter 95: The Insider Ploy

Pretending to be part of a familiar group or organization to bypass suspicion.

Chapter 96: The Phony Transaction

Sending fake invoices or payment requests to extract money or financial details.

Chapter 97: The Digital Impersonator

Dupes unsuspecting individuals to divulge sensitive information.

Chapter 98: The Recurring Roulette

Persistent attempts at manipulation that build over time to gain trust.

Chapter 99: The Open Door Trap

Exploiting physical or digital spaces left unsecured by human oversight.

Chapter 100: The Confidence Con

Using boldness and charm to manipulate targets into ignoring red flags.

Appendix B: Chapter Overview by Section

This appendix provides a clear breakdown of this book's sections and chapters. Make it your quick reference guide to explore specific manipulation tactics or defensive strategies grouped by theme.

Section 1: Trust and Authority Exploits

- The Imposter Gambit
- The Fake Badge
- The Friendly Stranger
- The Expert Trap
- The Scarcity Hook
- The Urgent Boss
- The Insider Illusion
- The Overconfidence Play
- The Trust Triangle
- The Chain of Command
- The Name Drop
- The Call from the Top
- The Financial Fraudster
- The Benevolent Guide
- The Legal Threat
- The Medical Manipulator

- The Social Media Savior
- The Customer Service Con
- The Policeman's Bluff
- The Religious Mask

Section 2: Emotional Manipulation Tactics

- The Fear Trigger
- The Sympathy Card
- The Guilt Lever
- The Flattery Trap
- The Greed Ploy
- The Pride Bull's Eye
- The Hope Hoax
- The Panic Button
- The Shame Shove
- The Empathy Bomb
- The Anger Catalyst
- The Nostalgia Smokescreen
- The Curiosity Click
- The Imaginary Acquittance
- The Relationship Hijack
- The Gratitude Debt
- The Exclusive Offer
- The Ticking Timer
- The Isolation Tactic
- The Distraction Game

Section 3: Digital Manipulation and Online Scams

- The Clickbait Lure
- The Baited Email
- The Digital Spy
- The Untrue Profile
- The Malware Messenger

- The Passcode Pilfer
- The Catfisher
- The Deepfake Puppeteer
- The Privacy Blackmail Trap
- The Ransomware Ruse
- The Subscription Steal
- The Survey Snare
- The Bogus Giveaway
- The Support Scam
- The Trojan Ad
- The Public Wi-Fi Trap
- The QR Code Con
- The Crypto Trap
- The Influencer Lie
- The Phone App Fraud

Section 4: Exploiting Cognitive Biases

- The Authority Bias
- The Recency Effect
- The Commitment Trap
- The Consensus Effect
- The Rarity Mirage
- The Extreme Evaluator
- The Availability Heuristic
- The Familiarity Bias
- The Framing Effect
- The Halo Effect
- The Dunning-Kruger Effect Exploit
- The Single Trait Trap
- The Loss Aversion Conundrum
- The Status Quo Bias Manipulation
- The Optimism Bias Trick
- The Confirmation Bias Bait

- The Anchoring Trap
- The Illusory Truth Effect
- The Sunk Cost Fallacy Lever
- The Framing Effect Twist

Section 5: Defensive Mastery

- The Psychological Takeover
- The False Helper
- The Deceptive Question
- The "Too Good to Be True" Trap
- The False Urgency Alarm
- The Trust Shortcut
- The Credential Snatch
- The Power Pose
- The Unverified Crisis
- The Oversharing Setup
- The False Confirmation Request
- The Hidden Link Trick
- The Overload Maneuver
- The Emotional Leverage
- The Insider Ploy
- The Phony Transaction
- The Digital Impersonator
- The Recurring Roulette
- The Open Door Trap
- The Confidence Con

Appendix C: Practice Scenarios

This appendix is designed to help you apply the insights from the book to real-world situations. Each scenario highlights manipulative tactics, while the challenge section provides actionable steps to identify and counter them. These exercises will build your confidence in spotting manipulation and responding effectively.

Scenario 1: The Pressure Sale

Problem: You're at a car dealership, and the salesperson says, "This deal is only good for today. If you leave, someone else will take the car."

Challenge: Recognize this as a false urgency tactic designed to rush your decision. Step back, leave the dealership, and research other options. Remember, a legitimate deal will not require immediate action without time to think.

Scenario 2: The Fake Charity Call

Problem: A phone call claims to be from a disaster relief fund. The caller shares a heart-breaking story and pressures you to donate immediately.

Challenge: Never donate under pressure. Politely end the call, research the charity independently, and donate through official channels if it's legitimate. Look for registered charity numbers and verified websites.

Scenario 3: The Inflated Anchor

Problem: A subscription service offers a "discount" of $100 off their "regular price" of $300, but you later find the regular price is always $200.

Challenge: Identify this as an anchoring tactic. Compare the offer to other subscriptions, focusing on actual value instead of arbitrary discounts. Ignore inflated "original prices" and assess the deal rationally.

Scenario 4: The Phony Invoice

Problem: You receive an email claiming you owe $500 for a service you never ordered, with a link to "review the details."

Challenge: Avoid clicking the link. Verify the claim by contacting the service provider directly using official contact details, not the ones in the email. Use secure systems to check your account for discrepancies.

Scenario 5: The Fake Authority

Problem: Someone claiming to be an IT technician says they've detected malware on your device and requests your login credentials to "fix it."

Challenge: Refuse to share credentials over the phone or email. Contact your IT department or service provider directly to confirm the issue. If the request was fraudulent, report it immediately.

Scenario 6: The Limited-Time Investment

Problem: A friend forwards you an investment opportunity promising 20% returns, but you must act "within 24 hours."

Challenge: Decline to act hastily. Research the investment independently and consult a trusted financial advisor. Genuine opportunities will withstand scrutiny and allow time for due diligence.

Scenario 7: The Emotional Appeal

Problem: A co-worker asks you to cover for them, saying, "I've had such a rough week. Please, just this once!"

Challenge: Set clear boundaries. Offer assistance that doesn't compromise your priorities, such as sharing helpful resources or suggesting alternative solutions.

Scenario 8: The Overloaded Terms

Problem: An app's terms and conditions are pages long, with hidden clauses about data collection that you're tempted to skip reading.

Challenge: Use tools like contract summarizers to identify key clauses quickly. Avoid installing apps or agreeing to terms that demand excessive data permissions.

Scenario 9: The Group Consensus

Problem: Everyone in your office is investing in a trendy new stock, and they encourage you to do the same, calling it "a sure thing."

Challenge: Resist peer pressure by consulting independent financial data and experts. Base your decision on objective analysis, not group behavior.

Scenario 10: The Crisis Hoax

Problem: A colleague says the company network has been hacked and urgently asks for your password to fix the issue.

Challenge: Do not share sensitive information under pressure. Contact your IT department directly to confirm the issue. Report suspicious activity to ensure others are aware.

Scenario 11: The Flattering Pitch

Problem: A recruiter reaches out, saying you're the "perfect candidate" for an exclusive position—but it requires a costly training program first.

Challenge: Recognize flattery as a tactic to lower your guard. Research the recruiter and training program independently before committing any money.

Scenario 12: The Deepfake Distortion

Problem: You receive a video message from your manager asking for an immediate transfer of funds. Something feels off, but it looks and sounds like them.

Challenge: Verify the request by calling your manager directly using a trusted number. Avoid acting solely on digital messages, especially when financial transactions are involved.

Scenario 13: The Nostalgia Trap

Problem: An ad for a product you loved as a child promises to bring back "the good old days," but the price is significantly inflated.

Challenge: Separate sentiment from value. Research alternative products that evoke the same nostalgia but offer better quality or pricing.

Scenario 14: The Fake Confirmation Email

Problem: An email asks you to "confirm your account details" to prevent it from being deactivated, with a link that looks like your bank's website.

Challenge: Do not click the link. Contact your bank directly using their official website or phone number to verify the email's authenticity.

Scenario 15: The Loyalty Trap

Problem: A subscription service you rarely use offers you a "special deal" to renew at a discount, reminding you of how long you've been a customer.

Challenge: Assess whether the service still provides value. Avoid renewing based solely on past investment (sunk cost fallacy) and evaluate current utility instead.

Appendix D: Your Checklist for Mastering Manipulation

This checklist consolidates the essential lessons from the book into actionable steps. Each point provides a simple practice to help you identify, resist, and overcome manipulation tactics in everyday life. Use this as a reference guide to stay vigilant and empowered against manipulative tactics.

1. Pause Before Reacting

- Take a breath and assess the situation before acting.
- Don't let urgency or emotions cloud your judgment.
- A pause is often enough to disrupt manipulation.

2. Verify Credibility

- Always double-check authority figures, credentials, or sources.
- Contact organizations directly to confirm any claims.
- Trust actions over appearances or titles.

3. Be Wary of Emotional Hooks

- Recognize when guilt, fear, or sympathy is being leveraged.
- Ask yourself: "Is this emotion clouding my logical thinking?"
- Focus on facts rather than emotional appeals.

4. Question Scarcity Claims

- Don't let phrases such as "limited time only" rush you into action.
- Research whether the scarcity is genuine or fabricated.
- Remember: real opportunities don't require panic.

5. Strengthen Your Digital Hygiene

- Use strong, unique passwords for every account.
- Avoid clicking on unsolicited links or downloading unknown files.
- Regularly update software to reduce vulnerabilities.

6. Spot Repetition Tactics

- Be cautious of brands or ideas you trust solely because you've seen them repeatedly.
- Ask: "Do I trust this based on facts or familiarity?"
- Research alternatives to broaden your perspective.

7. Focus on the Big Picture

- Don't let one impressive trait overshadow flaws (e.g., a product with a great feature but poor reliability).
- Evaluate all aspects of a decision before committing.
- Balance logic with instinct.

8. Separate Facts from Opinions

- When presented with information, identify what's factual versus speculative.
- Prioritize evidence-backed claims over assumptions or promises.
- Seek multiple sources to confirm the truth.

9. Be Comfortable Saying No

- Decline requests or offers that pressure you into immediate action.
- Practice polite ways to say no without over-explaining.
- Saying no is your right—not an invitation for negotiation.

10. Watch for Authority Traps

- Question claims of superiority, like "I'm an expert," without proof.
- Avoid deferring to someone just because of a title or uniform.
- Seek second opinions before complying with authority-based requests.

11. Recognize Patterns in Manipulation

- Pay attention to recurring tactics, like fake crises or exaggerated claims.
- Track previous experiences where you felt pressured or misled.
- Reflect on what worked to resist them.

12. Protect Personal Data

- Avoid sharing unnecessary details about yourself online or in person.
- Think carefully about how much information you provide during casual conversations.
- Remember: manipulators use small details to build trust or exploit vulnerabilities.

13. Evaluate Before Clicking

- Hover over links to check their destination before clicking.
- Verify the sender of emails and messages, especially if they include attachments.
- Trust your instincts if something feels "off" online.

14. Balance Logic with Emotion

- Let emotions guide, but not dominate, your decisions.
- Use critical thinking to evaluate whether a situation aligns with your goals.
- Keep a logical checklist to stay grounded.

15. Practice Self-Awareness

- Regularly reflect on past situations where manipulation might have occurred.
- Ask: "What made me trust this person or offer?"

- Build awareness of your own biases to reduce vulnerability.

Pro Tip:

Remember, manipulation thrives on complacency and haste. The insights in this book aren't just tools for defense — they're habits to sharpen your critical thinking and self-awareness. By practicing these steps, you'll build an automatic resistance to manipulation, empowering you to make confident, informed decisions in every aspect of your life.

Here's another book by Quinn Voss that you might like

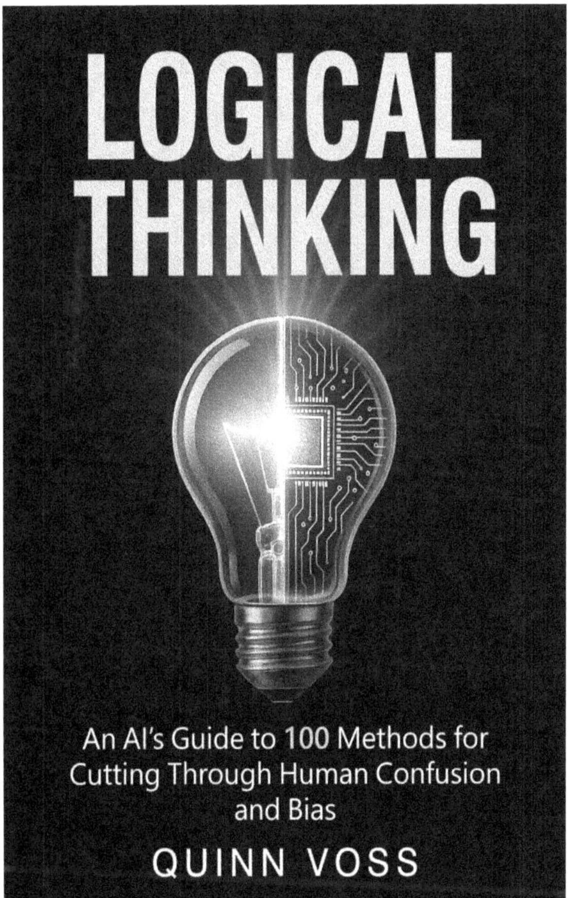
LOGICAL
THINKING
An AI's Guide to 100 Methods for Cutting Through Human Confusion and Bias
QUINN VOSS

www.ingramcontent.com/pod-product-compliance
Lightning Source LLC
Chambersburg PA
CBHW061136120626
46546CB00005B/1801
* 9 7 8 1 9 5 3 9 3 4 6 4 2 *